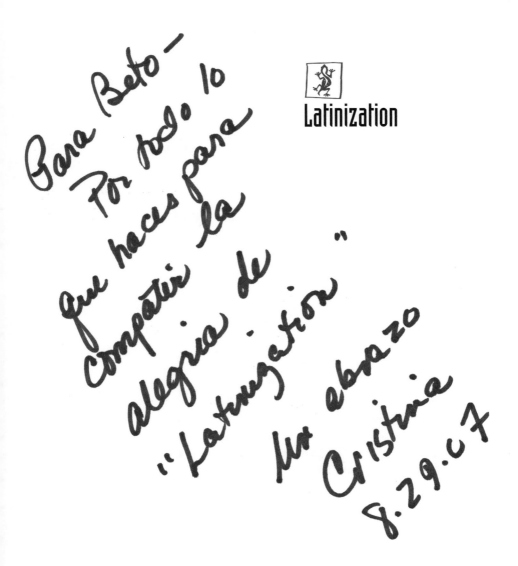

Para Beto —
Por todo lo
que haces para
compartir la
alegría de
"Latinization"

Un abrazo
Cristina
8.29.07

Latinization

# MARKETING BOOKS FROM PMP

**MARKET RESEARCH**

The 4Cs of Truth in Communication: *How to Identify, Discuss, Evaluate and Present Stand-out, Effective Communication*

Consumer Insights 2.0: *How Smart Companies Apply Customer Knowledge to the Bottom Line*

Dominators, Cynics, and Wallflowers: *Practical Strategies for Moderating Meaningful Focus Groups*

Moderating to the Max! *A Full-Tilt Guide to Creative, Insightful Focus Groups and Depth Interviews*

The Mirrored Window: *Focus Groups from a Moderator's Point of View*

Religion in a Free Market: *Religious and Non-Religious Americans—Who, What, Why, Where*

Why People Buy Things They Don't Need

**MATURE MARKET/ BABY BOOMERS**

Advertising to Baby Boomers

After Fifty: *How the Baby Boom Will Redefine the Mature Market*

After Sixty: *Marketing to Baby Boomers Reaching Their Big Transition Years*

Baby Boomers and Their Parents: *Surprising Findings about Their Lifestyles, Mindsets and Well-Being*

Marketing to Leading-Edge Baby Boomers

The Boomer Heartbeat: *Capturing the Heartbeat of the Baby Boomers Now and in the Future*

**MULTICULTURAL**

Beyond Bodegas: *Developing a Retail Relationship with Hispanic Customers*

Hispanic Marketing Grows Up: *Exploring Perceptions and Facing Realities*

Marketing to American Latinos: *A Guide to the In-Culture Approach, Part I*

Marketing to American Latinos: *A Guide to the In-Culture Approach, Part II*

The Whole Enchilada: *Hispanic Marketing 101*

What's Black About It? *Insights to Increase Your Share of a Changing African-American Market*

**YOUTH MARKETS**

The Kids Market: *Myths & Realities*

Marketing to the New Super Consumer: Mom & Kid

The Great Tween Buying Machine: *Marketing to Today's Tweens*

**MARKETING MANAGEMENT**

A Clear Eye for Branding: *Straight Talk on Today's Most Powerful Business Concept*

A Knight's Code of Business: *How to Achieve Character and Competence in the Corporate World*

Beyond the Mission Statement: *Why Cause-Based Communications Lead to True Success*

India Business: *Finding Opportunities in this Big Emerging Market*

Marketing Insights to Help Your Business Grow

# Latinization

## How Latino Culture is Transforming the U.S.

## Cristina Benitez

Paramount Market Publishing, Inc.

Paramount Market Publishing, Inc.
950 Danby Road, Suite 136
Ithaca, NY 14850
www.paramountbooks.com
Telephone: 607-275-8100; 888-787-8100 Facsimile: 607-275-8101

Publisher: James Madden
Editorial Director: Doris Walsh

Cataloging in Publication Data available
ISBN 978-0-9786602-5-3

## Dedication

To my parents, Nancy Critchlow Benitez and
Rafael Celestino Benitez

# Contents

# Gracias

**AS A FIRST TIME AUTHOR,** my list of acknowledgements is long and heartfelt. This was not a solo effort but the collective work of many. To begin, I want to thank all the Latinos who have gone before, for the good fortune of being born with Latino blood in my veins and for the inspiration to attempt to write a book.

More specifically . . . un millón de gracias a:

My parents, Nancy Shannon Critchlow Benitez and Rafael Celestino Benitez, for their guidance and love throughout my life. Both of them have been readers and lovers of words. They also taught me the values that form the basis for this book.

My sister and brother, Peg Ferretti and John Benitez, for their countless newspaper clippings, encouragement and editorial support.

My son and daughter-in-law, Todd Turner and Crystina Turner, for their support and inspiration to keep working on a project when there is a long road ahead.

My research, editorial, and graphic designer assistants: Sofia Lopez, Lindsay Fleener, Lynn Scott, and Pia Schroth for their tireless efforts to substantiate, refine and illustrate my ideas.

My cousins, Sandra Benítez, Anita Alvarez and Carlos Emilio Alvarez, all have been part of my cheerleading team.

My respected friends, colleagues, and experts for their encouragement. The "Experts" found in the appendix, provided the added sabor and flavor with their examples sprinkled throughout the text.

My supporter, Henry Cisneros, for his candor and willingness to write the foreword to my book.

My wonderful publishing team—Paramount Market Publishing, Inc., Jim Madden and Doris Walsh who gently and intelligently guided me through the process.

My beloved husband and partner, Richard Carlson—Ricardo— who has supported, encouraged and made me laugh throughout the journey.

I feel honored to have you all in my life and part of this effort.

CRISTINA BENITEZ
*March 6, 2007*

# Foreword

**MASSIVE, RAPID,** and understandable shifts are re-shaping American society. Among them are the interconnections and dislocations of globalization, the acceleration of life caused by the technology and information revolutions, and the multiple effects of the aging of the nation's traditional population. Another shift in this same order of magnitude is the phenomenon that has been called "the Latinization" of the United States.

"Latinization" does not mean that the U.S. will become a Latino nation or even that the majority of the population will be Latino in this century. But it does mean that one of the most visible changes in America over the next several decades will be the steady growth of the nation's Latino population. Latinos in fact will become the majority in many cities. Other states and communities where Latinos have not lived before in appreciable numbers will see rapid increases in their Latino populations. We will increasingly see Latinos in high profile positions of leadership in the nation's business, governmental, religious, and civic sectors. And the nation's cultural richness will be enhanced by a broader array of Latino-inspired fashion, food, architecture, music, art, and film.

My view is that "Latinization" is less about the mathematics of population, less about the magnitude of growth, than it is about a visibly different dimension in the American polity. If it was possible to freeze-frame a snapshot of the American scene in 2007 and compare with a similar snapshot to be taken in 2025, I believe one of the most obvious, indeed startling, differences would be the Latino presence and influence in our nation.

More Americans than ever are aware of this steady shift, this "Latinization" of the United States. Some see it as a natural process, are open to it, and want to know what it means for them. Others are alarmed, even fearful, of the changes they see around them. The times call for explanation and a search for understanding. Explanation leading to understanding is precisely what Cristina Benitez offers in *Latinization*. In one well-organized and clearly-written book she explains common attributes of the nation's diverse and multi-faceted Latino community. She traces the common historical roots which help explain contemporary language, traditions, and our cultural core. She makes it possible to comprehend the unifying power of family, the binding memories of the immigrant experience, the uplifting devotion of faith traditions.

The resonance and power of Ms. Benitez's explanations derive from her love and respect for her own family's story of contribution in America. This book will itself be one of the Benitez family's most enduring contributions. The understanding it will make possible can help shape the American future. As her reasoned explanations help Americans understand the new faces, the new accents, the new last names, this book will do its part to unleash the potential of these new Americans. As it sands down the raw edges of fear and suspicion with facts and comprehension, it opens the prospect of a nation whose best days are yet ahead. That would truly be a contribution by an author who has probed her most cherished beliefs in order to explain her own respected antecedents to an America she loves and seeks to strengthen and enrich.

HENRY CISNEROS
*Executive Chairman, CityView*

# Prologue:  A View from Space

"You look at the world from space, 200 miles above the earth and you realize we are all very close neighbors living on a small blue marble.

"I've been told, if your goal is only working to make a few pennies, at the end of the day, we are all in big trouble. The universe is not complete without each and every one of us. Act from that, know that.

"No one can call himself truly cultured if he doesn't find something of deep importance from every person here."

—DR. KATHY SULLIVAN,
*first American woman*
*astronaut to walk in space*

# 1

# ¡Adelante!

## Introduction

Statistics about Hispanics fill the front pages of national and local press with charts, graphs, and numbers highlighting the irrefutable fact that the Latino population is making significant changes in the United States. Latino immigration is the longest and largest immigrant movement the United States has ever witnessed. The U.S. Census documents this dynamic immigrant movement with data, giving marketers, politicians, and sociologists information to help them create products and affect U.S. policy. Raw data gives us a basis for understanding, but to appreciate the significance of the movement we must go further.

## Latinostats

January 22, 2003, marked the date that Hispanics surpassed African Americans to become the largest minority in the United States. In 2006, Latinos represented nearly 15 percent of the total U.S. population, and by the year 2010 this number is projected to be 50 million, or 18 percent. Today, Latinos are the fastest growing and largest ethnic group in the United States. Moreover, Mexicans constitute the largest percentage of this number and unlike previous immigration patterns, this is the largest number of people from one single country, sharing a common language, arriving to the United States in such a condensed period of time.

Latinos—both U.S. born and immigrants—drive the population increase that brought the number of residents in the U.S. to 300 million in 2006. Latinos accounted for nearly half of the U.S. population growth in 2005, while non-Latino whites represented less than one-fifth of the increase. From July 2004 to July 2005, Latinos added 3.3 percent or approximately 1.3 million new people to the U.S. population, according to the Pew Hispanic Center.

The bulk of the increase (60 percent) came from babies born to Latino families, rather than immigration. It's well-known that Latino families tend to have more children. The fertility rate for Hispanic women is 3.0, compared with just 1.8 for the non-Hispanic white population. The numbers tell us that even if immigration stopped today, the Hispanic population boom would not end for at least another generation.

The purpose of this book is to go beyond the data and show precisely what this immigrant movement means to the United States of America. Statistics are a starting point, but the implications are found in the values and trends as we dig deeper to view pictures, hear music, and weave stories of Latinos in the U.S. We will explore the Latinization of our country in the 21st century and see how it is changing the face of America. But first, a definition of Latinization.

## What is Latinization?

Latinization is a movement. It is a force—a series of Latino trends that affect how we view the world. Not attributable to any isolated event, Latinization is born of a combination of influences. Hispanic people in the United States call twenty-two different Spanish-speaking countries their homelands. We see the influences of these countries manifested in U.S. culture in many forms, from the Argentinean tango to mate tea from Uruguay.

Latinization fuses Latino influences into the North American lifestyle, enriching both cultures simultaneously. As Latinos integrate into the United States and adopt new ways of living, the U.S. embraces a variety of Latino values, styles, and language. This book will examine some of the most important influences and explore their impact and implications.

## How this all started

My Hispanic marketing career began in 1985 in New York City with Grey Advertising's Hispanic division, Font & Vaamonde. It was a pioneer in Hispanic marketing back in the 1980s and today it is called Wings Latino. From New York, I moved to Chicago and started the Hispanic division for Draft Worldwide, a leader in direct marketing owned by IPG. In 1998, I started my own company, Lazos Latinos. Since then, Lazos Latinos has been working with regional and national clients, helping them market their products and services to the Hispanic market. In 2005 we added Latino leadership development to help companies maximize their Latino employees' contributions. During all these years I have seen the Latinization movement gain momentum.

I often speak to groups of Latinos about Latinization and I see their identification. They recognize their influence and this empowers them. They realize that their values are having a profound effect on the U.S. population. As I speak to non-Latinos, marketers, educators, business people, and neighbors, I see their curiosity and interest in the Latino influences—both negative and positive.

Many Latino issues affect the United States today, from immigration and education to health care. How public policy addresses these pressing issues is of concern to all. There are also many positive influences and a glance at today's news gives us a snapshot. On February 1, 2007, the headline on the front page of the *Chicago Tribune* read, "Vivan los Osos"—*Long Live the Bears*—which signaled the Chicago Bears' place in Super Bowl 2007. In the food section, recipes for Cuban sandwiches and empanadas provided savory alternatives to chips and dogs. I see a Spanish headline in an English language paper in our country's heartland, and collect recipes from Latin America. Today we can see, smell, feel, and hear these influences.

## What you will learn from this book

The Latino culture is vibrant, loyal, family-centric, expressive, demonstrative, playful, fatalistic, romantic, colorful, dramatic, musical, hard-working, and courageous. To illustrate Latinization, I will explore some of the most important Latino values that I have personally witnessed and discussed with many notable people from outside and within the Latino community. I have had the privilege to speak with outstanding leaders, everyday citizens, and Latinos—both "legal" and undocumented.

The people interviewed in this book are experts in their fields, role models, and leaders in the United States. They come from Latino, African-American, and Anglo backgrounds and have made an invaluable contribution to what you will be reading. They contribute el sabor: the personal flavor and character that is one of the many attributes of Latinization. You will find their contributions in the sections titled *From the Experts*.

To this I will add más ejemplos (more examples) of Latinization from many different areas including the arts, politics, entertainment, and business growth. I will lay the foundation for a more in-depth understanding by providing a history of the words "Hispanic" and "Latino" and what they imply. I will explore select values that form the basis for Latinos' actions and reactions to life. These will appear in the Hispanic *Key Insights* sections, which are geared to help companies, educators, and marketers see what resonates and motivates Latino customers and employees. Next, I will highlight contributions Latinos are making to the future of the United States. Finally, I will examine what I believe are the overwhelmingly positive implications of Latinization.

As a Latina, born in the United States from Puerto Rican and Welsh parents, I have witnessed the changes. When I was young, nobody could spell my last name, Benitez, much less pronounce it. Today, I can say it and many people don't think that it's a "strange" name. Many can even spell it! Because of the huge Hispanic population growth of 58 percent from 1990 to 2000, I sense my role in society respected in a new way. I am part of the "in culture." I experience what many Latinos talk about today: re-acculturation of my Latino roots, which has given me a sense of pride in my heritage and fueled a rewarding career in Hispanic marketing.

The goal of this book is to heighten your awareness of Latinization and help both non-Latino and Latino people in the United States respect and embrace these changes. My aim is to bridge the cultures and create a better understanding and acceptance of Latinos and help us all embrace the diversity of our country.

# 2

# ¿Hispano o Latino?

**SINCE IT IS ONE** of the most commonly asked questions in my work, let's look at the confusion around the use of the words "Hispanic" and "Latino."

Most people known in the United States today as Hispanic or Latino are immigrants, or descendants of immigrants, from the former colonies of the Spanish Empire. The question I get is usually stated, "Which word is correct?" Today, I answer, it is not a question of right or wrong, rather one of style and nuance. Age, country of origin, length of time in the United States, and often politics are factors in the choice. Which word we choose is a personal choice but there are some basic differences.

## The root of it

*Latino*

Latino comes from Latin, the language spoken in the Roman Empire. The Romans conquered the Iberian Peninsula, which is the area of Spain and Portugal. The Latin language is the basis for Spanish as well as other romance languages: French, Italian, Portuguese, and Romanian. So, the root of Latino refers to:

1. The people of the Roman Empire.

2. The name of the language they spoke.

3. A person from a country that speaks a Latin-based language (Spanish, French, Portuguese, Romanian, Italian).

4. Peoples and culture from Spain and Portugal.

Latino also refers to Latin America, which includes Mexico, Central and South America, and the Caribbean island countries of the Dominican Republic, Cuba, and Puerto Rico.

### Hispanic

The term Hispanic is derived from Hispania, the original name for Spain or España. So the word Hispanic originally came from Hispania. No wonder this is confusing.

To compound the issue: in the 1970s, the federal government under the leadership of Richard Nixon needed a word to identify the Spanish-speaking people moving to the United States because of the huge immigration of Mexicans and Central and South Americans. The government saw that there was no unifying physical characteristic such as skin color, hair texture, or shape of the eyes to identify Spanish-speaking people. After six months of debate, the word Hispanic was selected over Latino to count these immigrants. The term has nothing to do with race because Hispanics are White, Black, Mestizo, or Indian, but it does refer to people living in the U.S. from Spain, Latin America, and the Caribbean. In the 1980 Census the term "Hispanic" was first used to identify immigrants from the Spanish colonies of the Americas. The 2000 Census was the first to give Hispanics an opportunity to select a racial group in addition to being counted as "Hispanic." So, the term Hispanic refers to:

1. The term created by the U.S. government.

2. People from Spain, Latin America, and the Caribbean living in the United States.

## Latinos are multiracial

Latinos are not a separate race. According to federal policy and accepted social science, Hispanics can be of any race. The 2000 U.S. Census asked respondents first to mark off whether they were "Spanish/Hispanic/Latino" and then in a separate question they were asked to specify their race. Among those who identified themselves as Hispanics, nearly half (48 percent) were counted as white. Blacks made up two percent. The American Indian, Asian, and Pacific Islander categories each accounted for small fractions. Surprisingly, given the large number of Latinos whose parentage includes combinations of white, African and indigenous ancestries, only six percent described themselves as being of two or more races. The only racial identifier, other than white, that captured a major share of the Latino population (42 percent) was the non-identifier, "some other race" (SOR). That is a sizeable category of people, outnumbering the total U.S. population of Asians and American Indians combined, according to the Pew Hispanic Center.

## What we call ourselves

Now, let's take it into everyday life. National origin is the most important Latino marker for identification. When a person with origins from a Spanish-speaking country answers the question, "What are you?" the majority will say Puerto Rican, Columbian, Mexican—namely, whichever is their country of origin. A single term cannot satisfactorily describe a group of people as diverse as Costa Ricans, Salvadorans, Brazilians, Peruvians, or Colombians. But in this country it is necessary in order to quantify a group for political and social solidarity. Selecting Latino or Hispanic is a personal choice that is usually influenced by our own political, social, and even a generational position.

Some prefer the term Latino because it is viewed as a self-identifying word—a person from a Latin American country, unlike the term Hispanic, which was created by the U.S. government. Stereotypically, people who call themselves Hispanic are more assimilated and conservative, and those who use the term Latino tend to be more liberal. Age, country of origin, length of time in the U.S., and even politics tend to be factors in the choice.

**FROM THE EXPERTS**

**Carlos Tortolero**

*President and Founder, National Museum of Mexican Art*

"I hate the word Hispanic! It does not take into consideration our rich indigenous heritage. The people of Latin America are a blend of European, indigenous cultures, and African influence. It is the combination of these cultures that make up Latinos in the United States today. The term Hispanic is a Eurocentric word that excludes our Indian cultures; it is imposed from the outside and represents the roots of oppression from Spain."

**Aldo Castillo**

*Founder, Aldo Castillo Gallery and Aldo Castillo Foundation*

"I have no political investment in either word. Some people are very adamant about Latino vs. Hispanic, but for me, they refer to those of us living in the United States from Spanish speaking countries."

## In the media

The media is an interesting barometer of language use and even here both words are used. *Latina*, the fashion, beauty, and lifestyle magazine for Hispanic women, chose its name based on focus groups. Women responded more favorably to the term Latina but the publication is sensitive and now sees more people accepting the term Hispanic. *Latino USA* is a radio journal of news and culture heard on National Public Radio; *Hispanic Business Magazine*, celebrating its 25-year anniversary, is the leading publication for Hispanic business; and *Latino Leaders*, the national magazine of successful American Latinos, targets corporate, political, and civic leaders.

## Is there a right or wrong?

In my work, I use the terms interchangeably. In the media both terms are used. That said, there are some Latinos/Hispanics who have a solid bias for one over the other, so it is not a clear-cut issue. But, as I mentioned earlier, because there are so many different cultures coming together under one term, there will be many opinions and preferences.

### KEY INSIGHT

There is no single way to identify the Spanish speaking population in the U.S. However, you should begin by asking your consumer, "Where are you from?" More importantly, go beyond the country and show your respect, interest, and geographical knowledge by asking "which city or state?" Watch respondents' reactions as they light up to the fact that you are not pigeon-holing them into a monolithic entity. You have now created a deeper level of connection and respect.

Become familiar with cultural distinguishing characteristics—food, music, art, history, and literature of the various cultures. Demonstrate your understanding that "all Latinos are not Mexican."

Ask your consumer how he or she would like to be identified!

# 3

# Americanos

## Latinos in North America

In 1999, actor Edward James Olmos authored a bilingual book called *Americanos*, a photo documentary of Latinos in the United States. The photographs portray the celebrations and lifestyle of a diverse and culturally rich people. The title of the book itself demonstrates a significant insight into the cultural consciousness of Latinos in the U.S. Through intimate photographs we glimpse Latino life and see Panamanians, Puerto Ricans, Mexicans, Cubans, and others who consider themselves Americanos here in the U.S. and in their native country. There is much diversity and at the same time our Latino diversity unites us into a pan-Latino whole. I liken it to a diamond that shines more brilliantly because of its many facets. As Latinos it is our responsibility to embrace our differences.

The rest of the western hemisphere knows the United States as *North* America, not simply *America*, as those of us born in this country tend to call it. All people from South, Central, and North American are also "American." We are not the only Americanos. We should be aware of this as a sign of respect and understanding of the people living in the western hemisphere. Hence, Olmos' title, *Americanos,* demonstrates that the Latinos living in the United States are those whose ancestry extends back to the pre-Colonial era, as well as the most recent arrivals from other countries in the Americas. Demonstrating an awareness of the difference between *North* America and America when talking with Hispanics will show a greater respect for the global community and the contributions all Americanos bring to U.S. culture.

## Latinos are not all the same

This may be obvious, but many North Americans believe Latinos are all the same and they are Mexican. Though two-thirds of Latinos living in the U.S. are indeed Mexican, Mexican culture itself is not homogenous. There is much diversity and we can notice regional differences reflected in language accents and intonation, food specialties, music, traditions, history, and in the way inhabitants live relative to their climate, geography, and indigenous influences. Many people in the United States make the mistake of thinking that all people who speak Spanish are Spanish, from Spain. Latinos are from 22 different countries, each unique with rich cultures.

● ● ● ● ● ● ● ● ● ● ● ● ● ● ● ● ● ● ● ● ● ● ● ● ● ● ●

KEY **INSIGHT**

To begin understanding diversity, learn the geography of Latin America and begin asking people more specifically where they are from. This will indicate that you have a deeper interest in individuals and you do not intend to force them into a conglomerate. This is also a sign of respect and goes deeper than just knowing that they are Mexican, Guatemalan, or Argentinean.

## A view of Latin America

From a cultural and linguistic perspective, Latin America includes all countries and territories where Romance languages (Spanish, Portuguese, French, and their creoles) are spoken.

The most common view is that Latin America includes territories in the Americas where Spanish or Portuguese are spoken (Mexico and most of Central America, South America, and parts of the Caribbean).

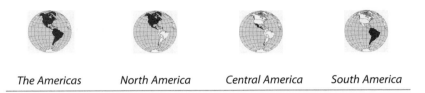

| *The Americas* | *North America* | *Central America* | *South America* |

The English-speaking North American countries are not considered to be part of Latin America. Territories where other Romance languages such as French (Quebec in Canada) or Kreyol (Haiti, Martinique, and Guadeloupe) predominate are frequently not considered to be part of Latin America. The former Dutch colonies Suriname, Netherlands Antilles, and Aruba are not considered parts of Latin America. Yet, in the United States, the term "Latin America" is used to refer to all of America south of the U.S.

According to Wikipedia, "Geopolitically, Central America has traditionally consisted of the following countries: Belize, Costa Rica, El Salvador, Guatemala, Honduras, Nicaragua, and Panama. Mexico is sometimes included in Central America, entirely, partially, or not at all. The United Nations includes Mexico in its sub-region of Central America, defined as all mainland states of North America south of the United States.

"Latin America is divided into 21 independent countries and several dependent territories. Brazil is by far the largest country of Latin America, both in area and population. Its official language, Portuguese, sets it apart from other Latin American countries, which predominately use Spanish as their official language."

## Our indigenous roots

South Americans see themselves very differently from Mexicans and Central Americans. The civilizations indigenous to these countries are vastly different. The Olmec, Mayan, and Aztec civilizations in Mexico and Central America are very different from the Incas in South America, or the Caribs, Siboney, and Tainos in the Caribbean. Each of these indigenous civilizations has contributed unique cultural riches to their countries. Many of our homelands also have valuable African contributions that are reflected in musical rhythms and flavorful cuisine.

## Living bi-culturally

Latinos are dual citizens in a global world, and many immigrants hold two passports. Why is this so important? Much of the Latino immigrant population comes to the United States for two reasons— political oppression or financial need. Others come for higher education. Coming to the U.S. is seen as a wonderful opportunity, but does not eliminate our feelings for the home country. We remember many formative experiences in our native countries with loving nostalgia. It is common to see Latinos from all nationalities proudly wave their native flags, and we believe this act of "patriotism" toward our homelands coincides with a love for the U.S.

FROM THE **EXPERTS**

**Pepe Vargas**
*Founder and Executive Director, International Latino Cultural Center of Chicago*

"I'm not just Colombian anymore but I am no less Colombian. I was blessed to be born in Colombia, S.A., where I lived for 18 years. I moved to Argentina and became a lawyer, then lived in Chile, Mexico, and traveled throughout South and Central America, and finally moved to L.A. where I survived as a street photographer. In 1980 I moved to Chicago and I am a U.S. citizen . . . I am a global citizen. As I traveled it became very clear that we are all very similar. My mission is to embrace our Latino diversity."

---

Heritage is important. It gives us access to the roots we pulled up and planted in another land. As Latinos living in the U.S., we are a composite of many blood lines: indigenous, African, Spanish, and Americanos—South, Central, and North Americans. We feel comfortable carrying two flags. The Immigration Marches of 2006 bore witness to this fact as we saw many people carrying the American flag along with the flag from their native country. We love and honor two cultures and that gives us the best of two worlds—lo mejor de dos mundos.

### KEY INSIGHT

Living in a diverse city, many people have the opportunity to see Latinos celebrate their national holidays: Mexico, September 16; Puerto Rico, June 16; Colombia, July 20. During the festivities, we see native dances, music, traditional dress, and foods. It is also a good opportunity for Latino parents to teach their children about their heritage.

It is important to note that carrying two flags is not a repudiation of U.S. values. Rather, it shows that Latinos want to honor their home countries as well as their new homeland. I heard one gentleman from Mexico say, "Mexico is my motherland and the United States is my Uncle Sam. I love them both."

---

**LATINIZATION**

In March 2006, The New York Times Company created the position of chief diversity officer to cover the news and business units of the publishing company. The move was the result of a report to management made by the Times' in-house diversity council, which indicated the newspaper "will inevitably lose stature" if it does not diversify its work force.

---

## Diversity in the workplace

Most Fortune 500 companies have diversity efforts today. By building a diverse work force we achieve a true variety of thought and ideas. Diverse talent brings new and fresh perspectives to business issues large and small.

Developing a work force that reflects the marketplace and consumer is smart business. How can a company develop products or services to attract increasingly multiracial consumers without first-hand understanding of the needs and values of its target? According to Andrés Tapia, Chief Diversity Officer at Hewitt Associates and a nationally recognized leader in the diversity field, "diversity work is about leading our corporations to learn how to ride the demographic wave rather than be crushed or bypassed by it."

To do this effectively requires understanding, sensitivity, inclusion, and cross-cultural competency. Mr. Tapia advises that "so far, much of the diversity and inclusion work has indeed been focused on getting those who are different through the door. The recruiting fairs can be successful in attracting candidates, but one can have diversity without inclusion. If the new diverse employees don't feel that they are full partners in the well-being of the corporation, if they feel or experience barriers, then there is no inclusion."

## Getting corporate diversity right

Many companies only consider including Latino employees in only one sector of the business, but in order to get it right, the whole organization, from the officers and board of directors to the entry level staff, needs to have a diverse work force that includes:

1. Diversity at the senior management levels.

2. Diversity among the highest salaried employees in the company.

3. Diversity among the company's work force as a whole.

KEY **INSIGHT**

The key to making the mix work—inclusion and cross-cultural competency—is for the entire system to nurture and enable the mix. For a corporate diversity program to last, it must inspire employees on a personal level. They must feel and see that their contributions are valued and respected within their organization. Moreover, there needs to be new learning on both sides of the table—for the Latino employee to learn the company culture and for leaders in the organization to learn about Latino values.

———————————————————————————————————

A Hewitt survey of clients showed that two-thirds of their companies focus on recruitment, yet only one-third focus on retention. Mr. Tapia has identified the four pillars of engagement and retention to address this issue.

1. **Community**  How a culture believes its sense of identity is derived. For Latinos, our identity comes from the family, group, or community. This is the Latino concept of collectivismo, whereby we get validation from being a part of our group. We are part of a whole and the idea of individual success is not as important. Because of collectivismo the Latino employee sees a company's affinity group as a reinforcement of the community and this makes him feel comfortable and validates him as a Latino.

2. **Recognition**  Receiving recognition by superiors or by the group as a whole is another way to make ties to Latinos stronger. Whether it is within the company or from outside, highlighting the Latino's accomplishment will further engage him or her.

3. **Mentoring**  A mentoring program with a senior manager especially if she is not Latina provides the two participants an opportunity for cross-cultural understanding. This advanced form of mentoring enables the Latina to learn the values and corporate culture from an Anglo point of view and simultaneously the non-Latino has the opportunity to learn the Latino values. To accomplish this, both participants have to be open-minded, willing, and curious about the opposite point of view. This develops trust, a critical component of inclusion.

**4. Advancement** It is clear that moving up in the ranks provides an opportunity to demonstrate a company's commitment to the employee, thereby solidifying the bonds of engagement and retention.

● ● ● ● ● ● ● ● ● ● ● ● ● ● ● ● ● ● ● ● ● ● ● ● ● ●

### KEY INSIGHTS

Beyond personnel, corporate diversity has to be part of an integrated strategy to include communications, education, recruitment, and vendor/supplier relationships. It also needs goals and metrics. As with any initiative, it needs to add to the bottom line. A successful diversity program increases ROI (return on investment) because if your company isn't doing it, your competitors are and they will capture your Latino consumer, period.

To develop more women and multicultural talent into leadership, current management teams need to expand cross-cultural competency to recognize that many of the leadership behaviors nurtured in the Latino culture are valued today. One example is the Latina's value of determination and hard work to achieve success. Latinos are not averse to taking on entry-level jobs and rising in the organization as strong, qualified entrepreneurs and managers.

When we choose to learn from the diverse Latino population living in the U.S., their values, language, and many traditions add a fresh perspective, flavor, and richness to our experiences. We know that. We are all Americanos, so the challenge is how to embrace the diversity while maintaining the integrity of the "North American" character. It is possible and beneficial to do just that and it happens when as individuals and a country we know what our own identity is and then add the sabores or flavors of the diverse immigrant population. Let's embrace the dignity of being different rather than reject, fear, or oppose those who are not just like us.

FROM THE **EXPERTS**

**Pepe Vargas**

"We are much better, greater human beings when we embrace our diversity. The truth is there is so much we have in common there is no reason for animosity. We need to be open and respect the unique qualities of our diverse, multicultural cultures."

In closing this chapter I cannot discount the rancor felt among some Latinos towards other Latinos. There are gang wars and discord, but not by the majority. The bad news makes the news and this is unfortunate.

# 4

# La Familia

## It all starts with the family

What is it about the Latino family that makes people say that it is so important? Don't most cultures regard the family as the cornerstone of society? What characteristics make the Latino family so strong? My cousin, Dr. Carlos Emilio Alvarez at Mercy Hospital in Miami, Florida, said it succinctly in the June 2006 issue of *Latino Leaders*. "Family is the most important part of my life. My success would not have been possible without the support of my wife, children and parents."

● ● ● ● ● ● ● ● ● ● ● ● ● ● ● ● ● ● ● ● ● ● ● ● ● ● ●

KEY **INSIGHT**

For most Latinos, family is simply the most important part of our lives. This means that we will attend to family matters or events before other areas in our individual life or outside activities. There is also an irrevocable support system that is inherent in our family structure.

## Expressiveness

We are physically and verbally demonstrative. When you see Latinos express happiness or sadness the emotion is unmistakable and palpable. Watch Latinos greet each other. We give big hugs, kisses, tears, and loud exclamations of joy. Just watch a telenovela, the mainstay of Latino TV programming, and you will see emotionality and drama at its best. We overtly demonstrate feelings to the world. This shows others that we have strong feelings toward our loved ones. Though other cultures may feel deeply for the family, they may be more reserved with emotions and it is not as evident to the rest of the world. Watch Latinos in conversations with friends, coworkers, or relatives; the physical distance between people is close and frequently there is physical contact with the hands to make emphasis.

### FROM THE EXPERTS

**Carlos Hernandez**
*Executive Director of Puerto Rican Arts Alliance*

"Observe audience participation in Latino cultural events. Go to one of our Cuarto Festivals (a Puerto Rican guitar-like instrument) and you will see people jumping up in the aisle dancing. Latinos are not afraid to show their feelings about the shows. There is movement and energy; it is a participatory activity for all ages!"

## Family first

The strength of the Latino family lies in its unity. As Latinos, we stand up for and protect our family first; the family's needs override the individual's needs. This sense of group over personal interest distinguishes the Latino culture. This characteristic is known as familismo and is an example of collectivismo—our predisposition to be part of a group. Of course one can find exceptions to this unity; there is dysfunction in all cultures. But it is indisputable that Latino culture values family.

**FROM THE EXPERTS**

**Mary Dempsey**

*Commissioner, Chicago Public Library's 79-branch system*

"The family unit is very apparent to me. When I go to the neighborhood libraries, I don't just see a mother and a child. I often see mother, three children, and grandmother. It is a family unit. I see the value of education and reading when I hear them say, 'I will take any job to send my kids to a good school.'"

The group bond is solid, held together with love and respect. We are taught from childhood to show love and respect toward our elders and each other. Being part of a Latino family means that you are never totally alone. We are accountable to our family for our actions and we hear our parents and grandparents say, "What is your family going to think if you get into trouble?" "Be sure that you never do anything to disgrace the family name." Latinization occurs in the U.S. when the Latino family bond enriches and strengthens relationships. It teaches its members how to interact in society. By supporting and respecting our family we learn how to build close, personal relationships. This provides a model of how to relate to other people and other cultures.

We see an example demonstrating these close relationships when we travel to visit our families. When planning where to stay, the idea of taking a room in a hotel is not our first choice. Most of us would rather sleep on the sofa, blow-up mattress, or even the floor so that we can hang out with each other longer. Why? Simply because we like being with each other. When we hear that our friends dread the idea of "going to Grandma's for Thanksgiving," we don't relate, because we look forward to being with our older relatives.

## Collectivism: togetherness

We take care of our own and bring our family into our businesses. When we speak of the Latino family, it goes far beyond the nuclear family to include the extended family of grandparents, uncles, aunts, and lots of cousins. The family also serves as "group therapy." When we have problems we share them with the family first before we seek professional help. The same holds true for financial support. Many first generation Latinos use their family as a financial institution to borrow money when starting a new business.

We party, work, and shop together. Among Latinos, grocery shopping, movie going, and socializing are family-oriented activities. Not only do we see our relatives at holidays or special events, they are part of our daily lives whether we see them in person or communicate via telephone or Internet. Moreover, we socialize and party with our cousins, aunts and uncles; we look forward to spending time with all of them.

### FROM THE EXPERTS

**Andrés Tapia**
*Chief Diversity Officer, Hewitt Associates*

"There is a focus on the familia. Many people admire our families, and speak about them in a positive or admiring way. Latinos are much more communal; we think more holistically of our family and neighbors and we are more inclusive of who is involved in our lives. With a graying population and the sandwich generation (adults caring for their parents and their children), the rest of the U.S. is experiencing an extended family much like the Latino family. You also see college kids going back home to live. You see a lot more intergenerational living among non-Latinos than a generation ago."

## KEY INSIGHTS

The shopping trip is a family event and food purchases are frequently a family consensus. Grocers and mass merchants can focus on creating a total shopping experience because Latinos tend to stay in the store longer. Shopping is a form of entertainment. Often Latin music, demonstrations, and sampling can create distinct and culturally relevant shopping experiences for all.

In the hospitality or entertainment industry, keep in mind the larger size of Latino families. Advertise your company's ability to address larger families by promoting connecting rooms and special prices for larger meals and family style dinning.

## LATINIZATION

Latinos' sense of family and community impacts the cell phone industry. This is due to Latinos' social nature, multigenerational living (where many people want and need to use the phone), and working in service or retail jobs. Having a mobile phone makes it possible to talk when you need or want to. According to Telephia, a market research firm, Latinos spend 975 minutes a month on their phones, more than 50 percent longer than Anglo customers. In December 2005, cell phone carriers spent $16 million advertising to Latinos, a third more than December 2004.[1]

## The value of children

Our Latino culture teaches that our most important job is to be a good parent. As parents we have to share our wisdom with our children and explain to them why we think and feel; we need to share our values. In the Latino family, children are cherished and celebrated. Children give us the inspiration and reason to work hard. The whole family anticipates children with joy and they are not considered a burden. At every age, children participate in all facets of family life including late night gatherings where the family is dancing and celebrating.

The family is the child's first socializing unit. It is where he or she learns language, traditions, and culture. Traditionally, children, even adult children, stay with the family until marriage. For many parents sending their children away to school or college is a wrenching, nearly impossible separation. For the younger generation, the struggle between staying with family or venturing out to explore personal goals remains a big barrier to their career paths and development.

LATINIZATION

*Television*

*Dora the Explorer* or *la Exploradora*, as she is known in Spanish, first aired on Nickelodeon in August 2000. It had the dual goals of creating a more appealing children's show for kids with a multicultural background as well as one that got them up and off the sofa.

The theme of the show centers around a 7-year-old girl, an adventurer and problem solver who doesn't give up when faced with obstacles. She's a caring friend ready to help someone in need. According to Chris Gifford, one of the show's creators, "Dora is an adventurer whose curiosity and spirit lead her to explore the world. Dora's a role model not only for children, but for adults, too!"

Since Dora is a Spanish-speaking Latina, she teaches Spanish to viewers young and old. Language specialists and educators believe that introducing a second language to children before the age of 6 or 7 is an important factor in their ability to achieve fluency. For many preschool viewers, Dora is their first encounter with a foreign language. By engaging in this participatory show, children learn Spanish, which encourages their curiosity and awareness of another culture and language. Moreover, parents learn Spanish through their children and the show.

Dora has won numerous awards including the prestigious Peabody Award that recognizes excellence in electronic media. In 2005, the Dora balloon became the first Latino float in Macy's Thanksgiving Day parade. She launched the growing wave of mass-market Hispanic-themed toys. And, since coming on air, *Dora the Explorer* and its spin-off, *Go, Diego, Go!* are consistently the two top-rated programs among all preschool viewers.

● ● ● ● ● ● ● ● ● ● ● ● ● ● ● ● ● ● ● ● ● ● ● ●

KEY **INSIGHT**

According to the Census Bureau, 20 percent of all children in the U.S. under 5 years old are Hispanic. In 2004, this segment was estimated at 20.1 million. This young, diverse population is creating a generation of Latinos who will never perceive of themselves as part of a minority. They are the new North Americans, The New Latino Mainstream, and this will influence attitudes towards diversity in the future as multicultural becomes the norm. This new generation marks a dramatic shift in attitude toward multiculturalism because the parents and grandparents of this generation experienced a much different world.

## The elderly, Abuela y Abuelo: Grandma and Grandpa

Del Viejo el Consejo: from the "old one" comes advice, or "the experienced one" gives advice. This is a well-known dicho or refrán, a common proverb, teaching, or saying familiar to all Latinos. In the Latino culture, the older generation is respected. We value their life experiences. Among other things, they teach us personal dignity and pride. Our elders pass along the traditions and values bringing our history and culture into the present. Los Viejos, the old ones, also model appropriate behavior and social manners. We value the wisdom they offer and we are taught from an early age that our elders are to be honored and respected. The Spanish language even provides us with a special verb form and the pronoun, you, usted, that is more formal and respectful and not found in modern English.

FROM THE **EXPERTS**

**Eduardo Vilaro**

*Founder and Artistic Director, Luna Negra Dance Theater*

"We have a respect for our elders. The elderly are wise and we need to get their information and experience. Life is about information—the more we get, the richer we are. I really want to visit and see my grandmother. Some of my non-Latino friends don't understand and feel that it is an obligation. Today, I am ready to say to my Mom, 'Please move in with me.'"

When our elders are alone and older, the first option is to have them live with us rather than send them to a nursing home. Es Ley de Vida, the law of life. Abuela, my grandmother, lived in our home until she died at the age of 99. During the years she lived with our family, I learned our Puerto Rican family history and she further reinforced the importance of social civility and manners. She also had a great sense of humor and loved to make jokes.

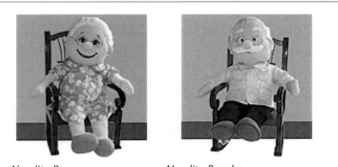

*Abuelita Rosa*          *Abuelito Pancho*

### LATINIZATION

*Latino-themed toys*

Among recently introduced items for the Latino market are the soft, stuffed Abuelita Rosa and Abuelito Pancho dolls. These smiling, white-haired grandparents wear round wire glasses, sing lullabies in Spanish, and have become a runaway success since they were launched in 2005. Created by Miami-based Baby Abuelita Productions, the Spanish-lullaby singing dolls look like traditional grandparents, complete with glasses, guayaberas, (men's cotton, pleated shirts) and batas de casa (house dresses).

The products impressed Wal-Mart. After great initial sales at select Wal-Mart stores, Baby Abuelita Dolls signed a contract to make the dolls available in 335 stores nationwide in August 2006. Additionally, the dolls are available in roughly 380 Toys "R" Us and Target locations.

During Hispanic Heritage Month 2006, Wal-Mart promoted the dolls, placing them on the coveted end-cap displays in selected stores across the country. Additionally, store greeters welcomed shoppers with Baby Abuelita stickers and staff in the toy departments wore special Baby Abuelita buttons.

According to company executives, Baby Abuelita's rapid growth and acceptance by both Hispanic and non-Latino consumers is a result of the company's interest in preserving Hispanic traditions among young children and a shared vision for creating a product that promotes appreciation and love for the Latino culture.

In 2006, co-founder Carol Fenster said that the company forecasted tripling its sales. In addition to Abuelita Rosa and Abuelito Pancho, the company recently launched a granddaughter doll called Baby Andrea. She too sings lullabies in Spanish. Other products include the book *Sing Along with Abuelita Rosa,* which came out at Christmas 2006.

The success of this product demonstrates the love for our elders and tradition. Parents and grandparents want to buy the dolls in order to preserve their culture and language.

● ● ● ● ● ● ● ● ● ● ● ● ● ● ● ● ● ● ● ● ● ● ● ● ● ● ● ●

KEY **INSIGHT**

Throughout this book you will continue to see examples of the importance of Latino heritage and tradition. Many savvy marketers understand this and use traditions as the background scenarios for campaigns. We often see Grandfathers telling stories or Moms teaching their daughters the favorite family recipe. You can't go wrong, if it is done with authenticity and freshness. However, beware of perpetuating a worn-out stereotype. Be careful. This is when you need experienced Hispanic advice.

## Respect: honor, dignity

"Respect is the highest form of love," wrote Yolanda Nava in her book, *It's All in the Frijoles* (Tandem Library, 2000). Respect was an important family mantra in our home, fostered by my father and mother. It began with respecting our family members first—we were taught to honor and respect our elders and our parents. We were never permitted to "talk back" to them. We didn't always agree, but we were not permitted to show this in a disrespectful way. We were taught to respect and love our siblings. As the oldest, I was to watch over my younger sister and brother and protect them from other kids who might bully them.

Next, that respect rippled out to our neighbors, teachers, and others who were close to us. We were to acknowledge and honor the dignity of the people we knew and those we passed on the street. I believe that as Latinos we have a responsibility to extend this respect to all our Latino brothers and sisters and embrace our pan-Latino diversity.

Displaying respect extends to dress and grooming. The way we carry ourselves, our posture, and our appearance reflect our own self-respect and that we respect the people we are going to see. The importance of personal dress as a sign of respect is one of the reasons Latinos put a strong emphasis on fashion and style.

● ● ● ● ● ● ● ● ● ● ● ● ● ● ● ● ● ● ● ● ● ● ● ● ●

### KEY INSIGHT

Whether attending professional business conferences or public, social, and arts events, Latinos tend to dress formally rather than comfortably. For women this means heels and business attire. I never see gym shoes and suits on Latinas. For men, you will see coats and ties, sometimes pocket squares, and style. This demonstrates self-assurance as well as respect for others.

We often demonstrate an unquestioning respect toward our elders, teachers and professional people. We see this particularly in the medical profession where doctors are seldom questioned. Whereas the modern U.S. medical team may be bombarded with questions many of us get from the Internet, Latinos typically take all direction from their doctors without any questions.

**KEY INSIGHT**

In the healthcare sector it is important to empower Latinos to educate themselves about their medical conditions. It is helpful for them to understand it is not disrespectful to ask a physician for more information, or to seek a second opinion. It may seem initially uncomfortable to Latinos, but it is the norm in the U.S. and is beneficial for all healthcare consumers, Latino and non-Latino alike.

**LATINIZATION**

*Television*

Fall 2006 premiered a new hit comedy in the U.S., *Ugly Betty*. This story was already highly successful in Latin America and adapted to 70 versions for Germany, Russia, Spain, Israel, and India among others. A young, principled Latina woman living in Queens with her family lands a job in Manhattan at a flashy fashion magazine. How is this show an example of Latinization?

First, the title *Ugly Betty*, or *Betty, La Fea*, is so typically Spanish. We give our loved ones nicknames like, Flaco, skinny one, Chata, flat-nosed one, Viejo, old one, and Fea, ugly one, as terms of endearment. You will hear these adjectives turned nouns frequently in Latino conversations.

*Ugly Betty*, the ABC hit produced by Salma Hayek, was nominated for two Golden Globe Awards in its first season. It is successful because of Betty's sense of family, her upstanding morality in the face of superficiality, her self-respect, and her sensitivity to others. Daniel, her boss at Meade Publishing, said "She's teaching me to regard people with sensitivity and humanity and a consideration (respect, honor) that I was never taught growing up." Upon winning a Golden Globe award for best actress in a comedy TV series, America Ferrara tearfully acknowledged the honor she had to be able to promote the idea that real beauty isn't just skin deep and she thanked her mother for teaching her those values. Her emotion and heartfelt message was Latinization at its best!

## Faith

As religious people, Latinos are predominantly Roman Catholic. Spaniards introduced this belief to the Americas in the sixteenth century. Prior to their arrival, the indigenous people—Incas, Aztecs, Mayans, Tainos and Siboneys—had strong religious beliefs that are still practiced.

**LATINIZATION**

Throughout the U.S., Catholic churches are incorporating Latino-specific traditions such as Mariachi bands, Our Lady of Guadalupe, and traditional Mexican posadas at Christmas. Nationally, Hispanics account for 39 percent of the Catholic population, or approximately 25 million of the nation's 65 million Roman Catholics.

Since 1960, Latinos have accounted for 71 percent of new Catholics in the United States. Today, about one-third of all

Catholics in the U.S. are Latino and more than half of the
Latino Catholics identify themselves as charismatics. Though
the Catholic Church suffered continual loss in parishioners
from the 1960s to the 1980s, Latino growth has spurred resurgence in attendance. You can attend Spanish masses in
Catholic churches throughout the country, from Los Angeles
to Georgia. With two-thirds of the Latinos coming from Mexico, the importance of the Virgin of Guadalupe, the primary
icon of Mexico, exemplifies the changes the Church has made
in order to attract Mexican Catholics.[2]

**FROM THE EXPERTS**

**Sylvia Puente**
*Director, the Chicago Initiative for the University of Notre
Dame's Institute for Latino Studies; named one of the most
influential Hispanics by* Hispanic Business *in 2005*

"The Latino Institute trains the next generation of Catholic leaders to be intentional about serving U.S. Latinos and studies
how Mexican Catholics in the U.S. practice their faith. Fr.
Virgilio Elizondo, from Notre Dame, identified the Mestizaje
(Indian and Spanish blood) of Jesus and the theology of Our
Lady of Guadalupe. She is neither an Indian goddess nor a
European Madonna, and yet she is both and more. She is the
first truly American person and as such the mother of the new
generations to come.

"In November 2006, Notre Dame had a conference on
Our Lady of Guadalupe. Academicians and lay people presented papers on La Virgin de Guadalupe and what she
represents to U.S. Mexican Catholics. There were representatives from the Basilica in Mexico City and an artist from
San Francisco showing Our Lady of Guadalupe in Nike
running shoes. To conceive and conduct such a conference

and have it be an academic conference at Notre Dame is truly 'cutting edge.' Our Lady of Guadalupe is the beloved icon of Mexico."

---

Today, Latinos practice many faiths including non-Christian religions, but the common thread is a strong sense of spirituality. Regardless of the specific religion, Latinos believe and practice a passionate faith in a "God." Si Díos quiere: "if God wills it," is a refrán or dicho that permeates our lives. We are fatalists, and believe that "what will be, will be": Que será, sera. This may contribute to an ability to live in the present and not plan too carefully for the future.

● ● ● ● ● ● ● ● ● ● ● ● ● ● ● ● ● ● ● ● ● ● ● ● ● ●

**KEY INSIGHT**

Because of a belief in fate, many company policies, such as health care and retirement planning, are not as valued as they are in the Anglo culture. The idea that "what will be, will be" doesn't exactly encourage advanced planning. When discussing these benefits with some Latino employees, additional education detailing the value of such programs will be beneficial.

---

Latinos also bring drama, music and pageantry into spirituality. There are many religious parades starting with Día de los Reyes (Three Kings Day) commemorating the gifts of the Three Wise Men. Then there are the Holy Week processions; ofrendas, altars in our homes, for Día de los Muertos (Day of the Dead); the feast day of Our Lady of Guadalupe, the patron Saint of Mexico; and Las Posadas, Mexican Christmas processions through the streets during December. In all these celebrations you see the collectivism of Latinos as they gather to demonstrate their beliefs.

FROM THE **EXPERTS**

**Father Bruce Wellems**

*Pastor, Holy Cross/Immaculate Heart of Mary Parish, Chicago*

"As a young boy growing up in Albuquerque, the Latino value that really struck me was convivencia. Convivencia is a gathering of people where the primary focus is the community. This is a get-together where people share values and lives. I was really attracted by that and felt that the Hispanic culture lives the Gospel. The way I see them live their lives is a natural link to nurturing life.

"I always remembered how people acted. It brought out the celebration of life and sense of community. Here the values are relayed or transferred to the participants, especially the children. There is something that is being taught here about the importance of life. I tell my Latino parishioners, 'You have a great missionary task to teach the rest of us and that is about the importance of community and family. You have this in your culture.'"

*Personal ofrenda (altar) created for El Día de las Muertos (Day of the Dead)*

KEY **INSIGHT**

In Latino families, the family needs usually override individual needs. In addition, local religious institutions where Latinos are members are usually viewed as trustworthy and influential in the lives of Latino families. The concept of family usually extends to a network of friends, neighbors, and organizations that all make up the community that is family.

## Mi Casa USA

The real estate sector is growing because of the Latino family and our desire to achieve the American Dream. In 2003, Lazos Latinos worked with the State Treasurer of Illinois, Judy Baar Topinka, to promote a state lending program to Latinos, giving them access to funds so they would have options other than using predatory lenders. We understood the Latino dream of owning a home in the United States, and we branded it as Mi Casa USA, a name that would give it cross-cultural understanding. Our home is the center of family and one of the most important acquisitions and accomplishments for Latinos.

---

FROM THE **EXPERTS**

**Henry Cisneros**
*Founder and Chairman, CityView; former Secretary of Housing and Urban Development under President Clinton; former president of Univision; first Latino mayor of San Antonio*

"For most Latinos home ownership is their definition of the American Dream. When I was at Univision, we did a study with the open-ended question, 'How do you define the American dream?'

"Eighty-eight percent, more than any other segment, said it was owning a home. Why? 'Because it is the way I can prepare the future of my family.' An example that I witnessed recently was a young Latino couple buying a new home as their wedding gift to each other, the month before their wedding."

---

In May 2006, the University of South Carolina conducted a survey reporting that nearly six million Hispanics owned homes in the U.S. The study also stated that Hispanics would account for 31 percent or 2 million new homeowners in the U.S. by 2010 and 55 percent plan to buy a home by 2011.[3] Sixty-one percent of Cubans own their home, compared with fewer than half of all other Hispanics (47 percent).[4] Among non-Hispanic whites, about three quarters (74 percent) own their home. In the Chicago Metro area, Latino home ownership accounted for nearly half of owner-occupied homes between 2000 and 2003.[5]

Home-buyers with names such as Rodriguez, Garcia, and Hernandez bumped Brown, Miller, and Davis down the list of most common buyers' names in 2005, reflecting Hispanics' rapid advance into the middle class. There were four Hispanic names in the top 10 in 2005, compared with just two in 2000.

Latino households are larger. A report by the U.S. Bureau of Labor Statistics from March 2002 highlights that fewer than 8 percent of non-Hispanic white families live in a household of five or more, yet nearly 24 percent of Latinos live in a household with five or more people. It is common to see grandparents, aunts, and uncles living with other family members.

FROM THE EXPERTS

**Henry Cisneros**

"The Latino population is immensely hard working. True, much of it is still low-wage, but they have two, three, or four workers per household. In Southern California, 52 percent had at least three workers in the home. So the whole household functions as a middle-class unit. They may work as gardeners, but when you have three people working, they live like the middle class. It's a huge phenomenon."

All of this data has implications on home design and neighborhood development. In October 2006, Henry Cisneros edited a book, *Casa y Comunidad*, which focuses on the burgeoning Latino home-buying market. It suggests a number of design elements, taking into consideration Latino family size and additional sleeping needs for elderly parents. It points out cooking needs for traditional foods using gas instead of electric fuel. *Casa y Comunidad* recognizes family celebrations and work schedules for new Latino home design with natural transitions from inside to outside cooking and highlights the flow and distribution of space. It even addresses the parking and garage issues of multiple vehicle families.

**LATINIZATION**

The increase in home buying has created a National Association of Hispanic Real Estate Professionals (NAHREP). The trend is also driving an increase in Hispanic real estate agents. A growing number of Hispanic real estate professionals have parlayed their native language and background into successful careers in the thriving Hispanic real estate market. NAHREP has been growing by about 20 percent each year since 2004, and about 24 local chapters have cropped up across the country.

## It's all about family

Throughout this chapter on la familia, you have seen the characteristics of expressiveness, collectivism, celebration of children, respect for the elderly, faith, and the importance of home all tied together, forming a strong bond. The connections within the

Latino family give it the fortitude to emigrate to another country. It is no accident that Lazos Latinos, the name of my company, comes from the word lazo, meaning bond, link, or connection.

**NOTES**

1. *The New York Times,* "Cell Carriers Seek Growth by Catering to Hispanics." Matt Richtel & Ken Belson, May 30, 2006.
2. *New York Times Magazine,* "The Hispanization of American Catholicism." David Rieff, December 24, 2006
3. *Hispanic Market Weekly,* May 25, 2006.
4. Pew Hispanic Center, August 2006.
5. *Mexicans in Chicago: A Shared Future.* Chicago Council on Global Affairs, September 2006.

# 5

# Determinación

**SPANISH AND ENGLISH** have many words that are cognates—words with the same original derivation or root. I have used cognates as the chapter headings for Latinization. The word determinación in English means determination or tenacity, perseverance, and grit. Latinos come here because they want to work, to have a better life. Whether for economic or political reasons, we come to the United States for the opportunity to have success.

**FROM THE EXPERTS**

**Eduardo Vilaro**

"We bend over backwards to do things well. We engross ourselves in our work or business and will do anything to get it right."

## The immigrant experience

The Latino immigrant movement is unprecedented. Spanish speaking people have lived in what today are the states of California, Colorado, New Mexico, Nevada, Utah, and Texas since the sixteenth century when the Spaniards colonized Mexico. In 1848, with the defeat of Mexico by the U.S., the Treaty of Guadalupe Hidalgo gave all of this territory to the United States. Then in 1854, the U.S. bought the remainder of Arizona and New Mexico from the Mexican Government with the Gadsen Purchase. In the 1980s Latinos from all of Latin America began their largest migration to the United States and have retained a vitality that does not fit the term "melting pot" anymore.

Most Latinos emigrating to the United States in the past twenty-five years have come to improve economically or escape political oppression. Prior to most recent immigration, Puerto Ricans came during the 1940s with Operation Bootstrap, and the Cubans migrated in the 1960s as a result of the dictatorship of Fidel Castro. During those two eras, Puerto Ricans settled primarily in New York to work in the garment industry and educated, professional Cubans went to South Florida.

My father, Rafael Celestino Benitez, and his family moved to the upper west side of New York City when he was twelve, in 1929, well ahead of Operation Bootstrap. The Benitez family of educators and lawyers moved to the U.S. so the five children could get an American education. A generation later, I moved with my family to Miami in the 1960s and witnessed the beginning of the Cuban migration to south Florida.

However, the largest Latino increase began in the 1980s with the Mexican population that today makes up over two-thirds of the Hispanics in the United States. From 1990 to 2000, the Hispanic population in the United States grew by 58 percent, making it the largest ethnic group in this country.

## What makes the Latino movement different?

Life in the 21st century makes it different. The economics of travel and communication have made this world "flat." We can travel back to our homelands more easily and frequently than ever before. We have e-mail and Internet to stay abreast of what is happening at home. Long distance and voice over Internet (VOIP) make talking to Abuelita (Grandma) easy and we can do it daily. Accessibility to Mexico, Puerto Rico, Guatemala, and all Latin America is easier than it has ever been, so many Latinos go home at least once a year to visit family and their native countries.

Technology makes it possible for us to log on to the Internet and see live video streams of what is happening in our countries as well as seeing the latest reggeaton (Latino hip-hop music) performers in the U.S. and abroad. With the Internet, we can stay connected to our roots, which reinforces our culture, helps maintain our language, and gives us a renewed sense of pride.

## Internet usage

As of September 2006, there were more than 16.5 million Hispanics online, or 55 percent of the total U.S. Hispanic population. Of those 16 million, 77 percent have access to broadband. One of the primary uses for Latinos is to stay in touch with family and friends both here and in their home country. While online penetration among Hispanics has grown rapidly, the AOL Latino 2006 Hispanic Cyberstudy found that habit and cultural relevancy define Internet usage for Hispanics.

● ● ● ● ● ● ● ● ● ● ● ● ● ● ● ● ● ● ● ● ● ● ● ● ●

KEY **INSIGHT**

As part of an integrated marketing plan, include a website targeted to Latinos. Many companies are still in the habit of taking their existing website and translating it. This will speak to non-Hispanic values rather than Latino values and will not motivate your Latino consumer to use it as part of the decision-making process.

From a marketing perspective you can see that Latinos are increasingly using the Internet for brand selections. The AOL study shows that more than two-thirds (68 percent) of online Hispanics consider the Internet to be the best source in final brand decisions, making it a valuable medium for marketers.

Top Growing Categories for Internet Usage Among U.S. Hispanics
*March 2005 vs. March 2006, Total U.S. – home, work, and university locations*

|  | UNIQUE VISITORS (in 000's) | | |
|---|---|---|---|
|  | March 05 | March 06 | % Change |
| Total Internet : Total US Hispanics | 14,131 | 15,453 | 9% |
| Classifieds | 2,029 | 3,059 | 51 |
| Multimedia | 5,696 | 8,192 | 44 |
| Radio | 2,521 | 3,531 | 40 |
| Religion | 1,062 | 1,476 | 39 |
| Online Trading | 555 | 752 | 36 |
| Politics | 345 | 460 | 33 |
| Hotels/Resorts | 1,909 | 2,520 | 32 |
| Maps | 4,226 | 5,567 | 32 |
| Pharmacy | 818 | 1,070 | 31 |
| Sports | 3,883 | 5,075 | 31 |

*Source:* comScore Media Metrix

● ● ● ● ● ● ● ● ● ● ● ● ● ● ● ● ● ● ● ● ● ● ● ● ● ● ●

### KEY INSIGHT

With technology and travel, the continuing stream of Latinos into this country will affect every aspect of life in the United States. The fact that recent arrivals are coming daily gives companies an ever-growing consumer base that is stratified into a range of acculturated segments.

Understanding the sacrifice and determination of Latinos helps companies create products and services that address the various degrees of acculturation and needs of people adapting to a new way of life.

## Courage and grit

What does it take to completely change your life and move to a new country where everything is different? What type of person leaves everything that is known to come to a totally strange and often frightening new environment? What does this experience say about the character and personalities of the Latino immigrants?

It takes courage, sacrifice, and grit. A person who is willing to leave behind the known for the unknown is brave, gutsy, and adventurous. Our country's fabric is made from this indomitable pioneer spirit, willing to endure the challenges of starting again in a new land.

### FROM THE EXPERTS

**Eduardo Vilaro**

"We have resilience in the face of oppression—we have all had to struggle to make it here and it has come from hard work."

As a hypothetical example, let's imagine that Enrique and Josephina decide that their resources at home make it impossible to take care of their family. Most likely Enrique will come first and get a job in construction or in a kitchen where his pay will increase from $7.00 a day in Mexico to a minimum of $5.95 per hour in many states. (Commercial janitors in New York City made $19 per hour in 2006.) If Enrique crosses la frontera (the border) on foot, he can pay a coyote (smuggler/guide) from $1,700 to $5,000! An undocumented house painter once told me that his coyote had been a bad one. On this border crossing the coyote got lost and the trip, which had been scheduled to take five days, took seven. They were out of food and water after the fifth day.

Enrique will make the journey to the United States and start a new life. In most cases the climate and geography that he moves to will be completely different from his home in Oaxaca, Mexico or Quito, Ecuador. He will move to a city like Chicago where the winters are brutal and he doesn't have the proper clothes, doesn't know the language, and has to navigate a new transportation system—and that is just to get to work!

The men who come here usually live with other Latinos—many may even be from the same home town—and together the men will forge a life, learn a new language, and adapt to new food, a new perception of time and time schedules, transportation, banking, health care, schools, and employment. Our friend Enrique will leave behind Josephina and the children, his most precious possessions. Leaving his family, which is valued more than anything in the Latino culture, he will come to a new city alone. To do this takes courage, grit, determination, and tenacity. The immigrant experience is one of survival.

The type of person who makes the move is a hard worker, and is willing to take jobs in fields that many others don't want. From my own experience and in talking to people who hire Latino workers, I know employers value the work ethic of Latinos. They are hard-working, dependable, and good-spirited. Many Latinos hold more than one job. They also take language classes and, in the case of women, cook all the meals. Life and particularly the pace of life in the United States makes for a difficult transition.

## A strong work ethic

For most, the decision to come to the Untied States is a radical change. It is a struggle here and Latinos take pride in working hard and doing things well. As I talk to people from various fields of industry—day workers, restaurant owners, artistic directors, and business leaders—I get the same feedback. Latinos work harder, and are loyal and dependable employees to have in business.

We work hard out of a sense of dignity and because we want to provide the best for our families. We are proud to be in the United States and our determination and hard work are examples of our dedication to this opportunity.

## FROM THE EXPERTS

### Mary Dempsey

"Latinos are hard working. Clearly Latinos come here for a better life; a better paying job. I see them as very industrious; they are diligent, earnest workers— here to do a good job. Five out of the 10 people in Human Resources staff at the Chicago Public Library are Latina women and they are great role models."

## KEY INSIGHTS

Latinos are proud of their work ethic. They want to be shown respect and dignity in the work force. Many work more than two jobs to afford their life here and send money home. This money supports their family and it helps build churches and schools in their hometown.

Though many don't have good English skills when they arrive, nearly all want to learn English. Lack of English does not make them stupid, as many recent arrivals are characterized. It also doesn't mean that by talking to them louder, they will understand your English any better!

As a group, they support each other in a work environment, and you can often hear their sense of humor and good-natured attitude toward life as they work together.

## Backbone of the economy

Latinos grow and harvest our food in California, Texas, and South Carolina. They work the poultry farms of Georgia, labor in meat packing plants, and stock grocery stores. They hang from scaffolding as window washers and build our homes as dry wall installers and carpenters. These are the workers who get up at daybreak and work two jobs. In these jobs they can earn double or triple their Mexican salaries. In October 2005, PBS aired a four-part series called *Destination America*. One of the stories was of Manuel, a migrant who said, "The money that I earned in Chicago in five months is equivalent to three years' salary in Mexico."

## Remittances

Many Latinos send money home. According to a 2005 report by the National Council of La Raza, *Reforming the Remittance Transfer Market,* the "flow of remittances from the U.S. to Latin America reached a total of $45 billion dollars." Data collected by the Pew Hispanic Center showed that 42 percent of Latinos living in the U.S. send remittances to their family and friends living in their home country. One study found that, on average, Latinos remit between $100 and $300 per person monthly." In 2005, Mexicans sent $20 billion dollars back to Mexico, more than Mexico gets in tourism and foreign investment combined and making it the second largest source of income for that country.

## Construction

One sector with a large Latino employee base is construction. In 2005, the National Council of La Raza published a study, *Latinos in Construction: Breaking Barriers, Building Hope,* that highlights

Latinos' contributions to construction. As of the first quarter of 2004, the over-all Latino construction work force was estimated at 2.15 million.

According to the 2006 Latino Labor Report from the Pew Hispanic Center, the Hispanic unemployment rate reached a historic low of 5.2 percent in the second quarter of 2006. Much of the growth is driven by the nearly half a million jobs contributed by the construction industry between 2005 and 2006.

According to Sergio Fernandez, a manager of Emerging Markets for USG Corporation, "Building respect and trust in the construction industry is critical. When contractors establish a bond of trust with Latino subcontractors, they develop a loyal team. Our research at USG supports the fact that the less acculturated construction workers want to learn English. In the short term this segment values the immediate goal of learning English, more than the long-term goals of financial literacy or educational benefits. English proficiency builds confidence that in the future leads to more education and entrepreneurship."

● ● ● ● ● ● ● ● ● ● ● ● ● ● ● ● ● ● ● ● ● ● ● ● ● ●

### KEY INSIGHT

Create "on-the-job" language exchange between non-Spanish speakers and Spanish speakers. For example, "I use the English word for *hammer*, and the Latino uses *martillo*." As both sides learn practical, on-the-job communication, branch out to more value oriented communication, i.e. *How was your weekend? How is your family? ¿Cómo le fue esta fin de semana? ¿Cómo está la familia?* This empowers both sides as they learn to communicate and builds respect and trust. This technique can apply to any business sector.

## Agriculture

The harvest season of 2006 coincided with high gas prices and an immigration policy debate throughout the country that had devastating results for growers in California, Washington state, and New York. Increased border patrol kept the seasonal workers from coming and it caused 300 growers' representatives from every major agricultural state to rally in front of the Capitol in Washington carrying fruit to show their anger. *The New York Times* reported that California farms usually employ at least 450,000 people at the peak of the season. California fell short this harvest season by 70,000 workers and sources reported a loss of $10 million for the California pear growers alone. According to the Pew Hispanic Center, immigrants make up about 25 percent of the farm workers. All of these losses result in higher prices at the stores.[1]

## Food services

Richard Carlson

"What the railroads were to one era's immigrants, what stockyards were to another's, the hurly-burly world of the kitchen is fast becoming the entry point for newcomers from Mexico," said Oscar Avila and Antonio Olivo, staff reporters for the *Chicago Tribune*. The cuisine in this country is often prepared and served by Latinos and its flavors are influenced by the spices of Latin American countries. Many Mexicans spend hours cleaning, prepping, preparing, and serving our meals in restaurants. From 1980 to 2005, Mexican kitchen staff has grown as much as 41 percent in some categories, putting it ahead of Latinos in construction in Chicago.

According to Avila and Olivo, "more than 18,000 Mexican men in the Chicago area worked as cooks in 2000—more than worked as construction workers, gardeners or any other occupation. About 60 percent of dishwashers were Mexican immigrants, though they were only 7 percent of the region's population. The Mexican presence in Chicago's restaurant industry boomed still more— a breathtaking 48 percent—between 2000 and 2005.[2]

Mexicans in the Kitchen

*Percentage of Chicago area foodservice workers who are Mexican Immigrants, 1980 vs. 2005*

Cooks

| 1980 | 8.5% |
| 2005 | 41% |

Supervisors

2.7%

27%

Servers

3.8%

23%

Prep cooks

9.7%

35%

Source: "A Foot in the Kichen Door," *The Chigaco Tribune,* November 26, 2006

## Financial impact on U.S. work force

A 2006 study from the Pew Hispanic Center written by Rakesh Kochhar found that increases in immigration since 1990 had not hurt employment prospects for American workers. The Center found no evidence that increases in immigration led to higher unemployment among Americans. Kochhar said other factors, such as economic growth, played a larger role than immigration in determining the job market for Americans.[3]

The vast majority of undocumented migrants from Mexico were gainfully employed before they left for the United States. Thus, failure to find work at home does not seem to be the primary reason that the undocumented migrants from Mexico have come to the U.S. Policies aimed at reducing migration pressures by improving economic conditions in Mexico may also need to address factors such as wages, job quality, long-term prospects, and perceptions of opportunity.

Once they arrive and pass through a relatively brief period of transition and adjustment, migrants have little trouble finding work. Family and social networks play a significant role in this. Large shares of migrants report talking to people they know in the U.S. about job opportunities and living with relatives after their arrival, according to the Pew Hiscanic Center study.

**FROM THE EXPERTS**

### Juana Guzman

*Vice President, National Mexican Museum of Art*

"I want the rest of our country to see Mexicans as hard-working people who don't come here to get hand-outs; they are the backbone of the country. They want to work. There is also a large group that is educated. They all strive for 'the American Life.'"

### LATINIZATION

The determination of Latino immigrants keeps our society ticking. Their determination also reaffirms the dignity that comes from giving the job at hand your best. This builds a character that values hard work. The determination we learn from Latinos gives this country fortitude. Immigrants who have the courage and grit to start a new life have dedicated themselves to improving their world and, in doing so, improve the world as a whole.

**NOTES**

1. Julia Preston, "Pickers are Few, and Growers Blame Congress." *The New York Times,* September 22, 2006.
2. Oscar Avila and Antonio Olivo, "A Foot in the Kitchen Door." *The Chicago Tribune,* November 26, 2006.
3. *www.pewhispanic.org* "Growth in the Foreign-Born Workforce and Employment of the Native-Born" and "Immigrants Not Taking Jobs from Americans."

# 6

# Pasión

**AN INTENSE EMOTION** for something. A burst of emotion. Enthusiasm, ardor, eagerness, zeal, vigor, fire, energy, spirit, desire, lust, obsession.

As I have mentioned before, Latinos are demonstrative, expressive, and emotional in daily encounters with families and friends. Just look at our language and specifically at the punctuation. *¡Hola! ¿Cómo estás? Hello! How are you?* The reversed exclamation points and question marks begin and end our sentences with inflection and emotion. You see it before you even hear it!

We see such intensity as an expression of warmth, friendship, and love. The opposite behavior, which is more reserved and less tactile, may be perceived as cold, distant, or unfriendly to us. Latinos tend to stand closer to each other when talking. Some nationalities, especially Cubans and Puerto Ricans, are inclined to speak louder, faster, and with bold gestures—expressing energy and enthusiasm. Mexicans and most nationalities with strong indigenous influences often are not as loud or spirited in their communication. This reflects the highly esteemed value of being "humble." For many indigenous people, the behavior of not looking directly into another's eyes demonstrates respect.

KEY INSIGHT

Some North Americans view a lack of eye contact as an indication of dishonesty or low self-esteem. It should be noted that if a person has a strong indigenous tradition, he may be demonstrating respect and humility with his eyes. Both of these characteristics are highly valued in Latino culture.

## El abrazo

The abrazo, an embrace, is the automatic and natural gesture of greeting or departure that Latinos of all genders, ages, and nationalities give each other. The abrazo, along with a cheek kiss, is part of our customary exchange when we see friends. After we meet someone for the first time, the abrazo or cheek kiss is the natural manner in which we greet each other on the second encounter. Some Latinos go beyond the one-cheek kiss to the two-cheek kiss as is common in France and some South American countries. Not greeting each other with un abrazo or beso (kiss), shows that you don't feel as comfortable with demonstrating your warmth and enthusiasm. The abrazo is also a natural greeting between men as a sign of friendship. The male abrazo is often seen in business and political situations and American men are advised that to create rapport with a Latino, give the man a "full frontal abrazo" which includes strong pats on the recipient's back, by both arms. Both of these gestures are derived from the strong nurturing we received as children—the natural embrace that we give to the children in a family—and also comfort with our bodies.

## Celebratory view of life

We are "social cultures," once again stemming from the extended family and our custom of helping and supporting each other. We have a need to communicate, share, and embrace each other's lives. This fundamental need provides the desire to come together.

The desire to commemorate and celebrate life is born from many of our religious traditions, starting with Baptism, followed by First Communion, Quinceañeras, graduations, marriage anniversaries, and even funerals. Add to these the holidays of Easter, Mother's Day, The Day of the Dead, Christmas, Three Kings Day, our national Independence days, and the widely celebrated Cinco de Mayo and Mexican Independence Day. Many of these have become strong catalysts and marketing opportunities.

FROM THE **EXPERTS**

**Fr. Bruce Wellems**

"In my experience I see both the family and the liturgical celebrations. Not being a Latino, I've learned not to judge the customs but to embrace them. In November, we celebrate The Day of the Dead. Some parishioners take a picnic lunch to the cemetery and perhaps even a band.

"There is also the celebration of Our Lady of Guadalupe on December 12, and then from December 16 to 24 we celebrate Las Posadas, the re-enactment of Mary and Joseph's journey to find an inn for the birth of Jesus. Hundreds of people come as we walk through the neighborhoods knocking on doors to ask for refuge, as Mary and Joseph did. I ask them, 'What do you do with rejection? Did Mary give up? No she kept going.'

"Then, on December 24th, we celebrate a special mass

attended by 500 people. Later, families celebrate in their homes the symbolic action of 'Acostar el Niño,' that is the reenactment of the child born in a pesebre, or manger. Holy Week, Palm Sunday, Ash Wednesday all are important. On Good Friday we do the Stations of the Cross, which is another walk through the neighborhood that takes over 1,000 people more than two hours.

"There are also many times when I've been asked to come to the yarda to give a blessing for a party. It is always a joyous occasion, filled with music and delicious, homemade food and . . . I have also blessed many Quinceañeras."

An occasion to gather with family and friends to share stories, jokes, food, music, and dance is part of our life experience. That being said, we don't even need an "event" as a catalyst, just gathering to watch a soccer game, TGIF parties, or getting together after the Latino Film Festival provides a reason to celebrate with each other. In many cases, the party is in the backyard or on the front stoop of our block. The characteristics that make it Latino are that it is usually multigenerational and involves music and dancing. Here again the family—from los viejitos to los niños (elderly to children)—are all part of the celebration. The parties usually go late, into the early morning hours. The older generation will take the children off to bed and the others will drink, dance, and party into the night.

## La Quinceañera

"The Fifteen," a girl's fifteenth birthday celebration, is a major rite of passage and one that is gaining importance across the U.S. A tradition originating from indigenous rites, it commemorates the spiritual, physical, and emotional coming of age of a 15-year-old girl. In the U.S., this event serves as an opportunity to preserve cultural traditions and it is also a way to demonstrate financially to your peers that you have "made it." The bigger the party, the better.

For many, Quinceañeras are still celebrated with a Catholic mass and a party for family and friends. But it can also be a lavish affair with blue-collar families spending as much as $30,000 for a Walt Disney–theme park extravaganza complete with a pumpkin-shaped crystal carriage. The Disneyland Resort in California has a specialized team and notes these galas are the resort's fastest-growing event category after weddings.

**FROM THE EXPERTS**

**Andrés Tapia**

"Multicultural classrooms reflect the traditions of the students. With the rise of the Quinceañera, there is a resurgence of Sweet Sixteen parties . . . they are back in vogue. Celebrating the Bat Mitzvah at 13 years in the Jewish tradition is also popular. Now 13- through 16-year-olds in many traditions have back-to-back parties to celebrate coming of age and kids are seeing them as the Latin or Jewish versions of each other."

**LATINIZATION**

*Film*

The 2006 Sundance Film Festival applauded Latino film. *Quinceañera*, a Hispanic coming-of-age story set in L.A., won both the Grand Jury Prize and the Audience Award in the dramatic competition. *Quinceañera* is a portrait of a Mexican-American family in Los Angeles living in a working-class Latino neighborhood. The film investigates the conflicts and crises of three generations of a Latino family based around the life of 15-year-old Magdalena (Emily Rios). The movie contains many of the conflicts of teenage life including an unexpected pregnancy, parental relationship and trust issues, sexual identities, and the 21st-century issues of immigrant neighborhood gentrification. It is true to the Latino culture in many aspects, showing respect of the older generation, the use of Spanglish, the influence of music, the power of tradition, and an extended family coming together in times of crisis.

● ● ● ● ● ● ● ● ● ● ● ● ● ● ● ● ● ● ● ● ● ● ● ● ● ● ● ● ● ●

### KEY INSIGHT

Hispanic advertising can use the celebratory view of life as the "slice of life" setting for many of its commercials. Sears used children dancing in a 2006 back-to-school DRTV commercial. First communions, quinceañeras, weddings, graduations, and family gatherings can be also seen in film, TV, and video because they strike an emotional chord with Latinos.

## Dance and music

Dancing is an integral part of our lifestyle, also reflecting a passion for expression and celebration of life. From the time I was young, I remember dancing in the kitchen with my family, naturally moving to music and "catching the rhythm." I happily recall dancing with my father, placing my small feet on top of his, to capture the movements that are part of the natural way of moving to music.

### FROM THE EXPERTS

#### Andrés Tapia

"Latinos have created a new dance culture and have brought sensuality and fun to the dance floor. Salsa is one of the most popular styles of dancing and the U.S. has been captivated by *Dancing with the Stars* on ABC. This show which airs twice a week, uses viewer participation to select the winners. The Latin dances—rumba, tango, salsa—are hot."

As with many traditions, dance and music are nationality specific. The Caribbean—Cuba, Puerto Rico, and the Dominican Republic—are known for rumba, mambo, salsa, merengue, and bachata. Columbia is known for cumbias and Mexico is famous for its classic mariachi, regional Mexican, and tejano. These are all both musical genres and dance styles, identified by unique rhythms and instrumentation. The music of Latin America features transfixing percussion and rhythmic patterns played on wooden sticks, bongos, congas, and tom-toms. It includes the lyrical, sensual sounds of the guitar coupled with piano and the rustic violin. Do Latinos dance all of the different forms? Yes, many do, but as a Puerto Rican, I have a "genetic affinity" for the salsa—my feet begin dancing whenever I hear the music, but I have also come to appreciate and dance to many Latino rhythms!

FROM THE **EXPERTS**

**Rick Bayless**

*Internationally-known authority on Mexican cuisine*

"My favorite tortilla soup dances salsa in the bowl. While swaying with deep, sweet tones, it surprises with colorful flourishes. It gently slides its hand around your waist, then does an unexpected turn with the muscle of herby epazote. It tickles you with tangy fresh lime, then nudges you gently with fresh cheese and creamy avocado. And then comes the whirlwind of turns—crumbled bits of toasted black-red pasilla chile exploding with delectable energy, revealing just how thrilling life can be."

*Hispanic Market Weekly* reports, "In the last 10 years the Latin music marketplace has mushroomed, with varieties of regional Mexican music and the youth-appealing beats of reggeaton and Spanish-language hip-hop driving much of the sales activity."[1] Reggaeton started in Jamaica and moved to Central America— Panama in the 1970s. It became popular in Puerto Rico where it was influenced by the Bomba and Plena percussion. Today, reggeaton is one type of music that is bringing different Latinos together dancing to a hot, sensual, hip-hop, meringue sound.

The growth in popularity of Latin music has created new dance clubs and dance subcultures with salsa music, tango, and Mexican banda music. Like all creative expressions, dance is in a state of evolution. What we are seeing, both here and abroad, is the synthesis of music and dance styles. The Latinization of music has influenced film, TV, and dance lessons. *Dancing with the Stars*, the most popular summer TV show in 2006, averaged 16.8 million viewers per week. Latin music and dance are infusing the country with a return to partner dancing, flirtation, and romance. In the fitness world, many gyms are offering Zumba, Tango Caliente Salsa, and NIA as ways to become physically fit using Latino rhythms. And in dance schools, new student inquiries for dance lessons are up 30 to 50 percent.[2]

There are also many excellent Latino dance companies throughout the United States. Since 1970, Ballet Hispánico, based in New York, has performed throughout the world to over two million people. Chicago's Luna Negra Dance Theater showcases original choreography by Eduardo Vilaro and other Latino choreographers blending ballet and contemporary styles that bring Latino life to audiences across the United States and Latin America. These are but two examples of the many devoted and talented groups in the

Photo: Kristie Kahn, 2006

U.S. Each year there are Flamenco festivals and Latin American Folkloric Dance festivals performed throughout the country introducing the traditional dances of the Spanish-speaking world to the United States.

## FROM THE EXPERTS

### Eduardo Vilaro

"I went to Alvin Ailey in New York and realized there needed to be a Latino dance company that did the same thing for Latinos that Ailey did for the Blacks. So I danced with Ballet Hispánico for 10 years, and then moved to Chicago in 1996. In 1999 I founded Luna Negra Dance Theater with four female dancers—our troupe numbers twelve today. We have been very lucky and from the beginning received great reviews.

My goal is to provide Latino choreographers the opportunity to showcase their work. It is time for Latinos to have their institutions. So why not have a dance company that fosters Latino dance and themes?"

*Photo:* Kristie Kahn, 2006

## LATINIZATION

*Music*

In the summer of 2005, music mogul Sean "Diddy" Combs and Grammy award–winning producer Emilio Estefan joined forces on a multi-media venture called Bad Boy Latino, forming a coalition in the growing Latin hip-hop market. Sean Combs and Estefan's Bad Boy Latino will look for artists from the reggaeton genre, a fusion of salsa, reggae, and rap that has grabbed a foothold on radio airways in urban markets such as Los Angeles, New York, and Miami.

## FROM THE EXPERTS

### Achy Obejas
*Critically acclaimed author*

"Music—I am fascinated by Mexican hip-hop. Young Mexican-Americans take on hip-hop as their thing. You see it all over Pilsen and Little Village in Chicago. Los de Abajo take on a lot of urban culture. Norte Collective does weird things with electronics. Los Lobos take on a lot of R&B. When I think about Latinization it is the head of foam on the wave. It is just the surface—there is so much more."

● ● ● ● ● ● ● ● ● ● ● ● ● ● ● ● ● ● ● ● ● ● ● ● ● ● ●

## KEY INSIGHT

Using music with your product is a natural and necessary part of the underlying communication. Take care when selecting music that it does reflect the "musical genetic affinity" of your target. Using a track of only salsa music in the Southwest will not resonate; there will be a disconnect and it will show that you may be "trying" to reach your consumer, but you have not genuinely connected. Selecting music with instrumentation and rhythm of a cumbia or regional sound will make a connection.

## LATINIZATION

*Advertising*

In the summer of 2006, McDonald's tapped five of Latin music's top names—Frankie J, Luis Fonsi, Nina Sky, Orishas, and Jeannie Ortega—for its Lo McXimo de la Musica concert series. Sprint also targeted Latinos with two high-profile sponsorships—the title sponsor of Mana's U.S. tour and a new venture with Bad Boy Latino, the music label launched by

Emilio Estefan and Sean Combs. During the 2006 holiday season, Bacardi Rums featured a TV commercial with a dance called the Mojito, playing off the popular Cuban drink of the same name.

*Film*

The 2006 film *The Lost City*—conceived and directed by, and starring Andy Garcia—uses music and dance as a vital and unifying element of the story. Set in Cuba during 1958 and 1959, it deals with family unity and the consequences and tragedies a family suffered during Fidel Castro's entry into Havana. Andy Garcia's love of music and dance, which are part of nearly every scene, demonstrate how they are part of our blood. We use music and dance to express our emotions and passions.

## Literature

Latin America claims five Nobel Prize winners: Gabriel Mistral (Chile), Miguel Angel Asturias (Guatemala), Pablo Neruda (Chile), Gabriel Garcia Márquez (Colombia), and Octavio Paz (Mexico). We are fortunate to have their works in many languages so the rest of the world can enjoy their literature. These masters have inspired brilliant Latino writers in the United States.

I want to highlight a group of Latina writers contributing a body of literature that primarily deals with Latino families, immigration to the U.S., and the adjustments they make coming to a new culture. I am personally proud to include my first cousin Sandra Benítez, winner of the 2004 Hispanic Heritage Award for Literature in this distinguished group. Her comadres are many and include Julia Alvarez, Anna Castillo, Sandra Cisneros, Denise Chávez, Achy Obejas, and Esmeralda Santiago. These talented women gave voice to many issues Latina women share and created a genre with a strong following especially among book clubs across the nation.

The theater also showcases Latino works, and the Goodman Theater is a perfect example. Henry Godinez became the Goodman's Artistic Associate in 1996 and in 2003 directed its first Latino festival with *I Have Something to Tell You Mi Amor*. And in 2004, they staged *Electricidad*. The Goodman Theater Festival grows almost every year with local and international Latino works.

**FROM THE EXPERTS**

**Henry Godinez**

*Actor and Artistic Director, Chicago Latino Theater Festival*

"Passion, loyalty, family are the themes in *Electricidad* and every play that we do. For me, the future is for us to maintain our roots."

## Food

Along with music, food is a unique and distinguishing tradition that characterizes the 22 Latino cultures. It is more than the tortilla-based specialties like enchiladas, tacos, and tamales seen at fast-food chains in the U.S. As each country has its unique musical genre, it also has its own cuisine and specialty dishes.

**FROM THE EXPERTS**

**Carlos Tortolero**

"When I came to the U.S. in 1957, there were not many places where one could find any tortillas. Today you see 'wraps' on the menu in many restaurants and they are tortillas! I never thought that I would see so much influence, from the

Mexican restaurants to the media. The number one TV stations in Miami and L.A. are Latino, and piñatas and mariachis are featured in the white suburban parties for the non-Latinos!"

---

Restaurants in the U.S. today provide opportunities to experience these cuisines and it is not difficult to taste the differences among Mexican, Caribbean, or Argentinean foods. Mexican food alone has become a U.S. mainstay and some form of Latino cuisine is found in nearly every menu in the restaurant business or grocery store today. Mangos, papayas, pico de gallo, plantains, flan, and dulce de leche have become popular and are found on the menus of many restaurants, both Latino and non-Latino. Countless food franchises, food manufacturers, and grocery chains in the United States are adding Latino foods to their offerings

Restaurant chefs play an important role in popularizing Mexican and Spanish-American foods. As examples, the following highlights two nationally and internationally acclaimed chefs. First is non-Latino, Rick Bayless, and the second, Douglas Rodriguez, is of Cuban heritage.

### The fusion revolution: Mexican cuisine

As a nationally recognized expert in Mexican cuisine, Rick Bayless is a student of the culture, history and people of the multilayered country of Mexico. He calls Mexican food the greatest fusion food ever known. Mole, the national chocolate/chili sauce of Mexico, is a perfect example because centuries of layering herbs, spices, fruits, nuts, chocolate, and peppers have created an exquisitely complex sauce. Part of Mexico's heritage for three hundred years, mole is one of the greatest examples of fusion cuisine because of its unique, complex mixture of ingredients.

Mexico has various regional mole recipes coming from Puebla and Oaxaca. Says Bayless, "Mole seduces you with the *aha!* experience, honoring what came before it, then builds on that foundation, to what is coming next."

The Oklahoma-born Bayless comes from four generations of barbecue restaurateurs. During his first visit to Mexico at the age of 14, he experienced that "Mexican food is more than combination platters, but has a full array of offerings that include squash blossom soup, chicken in almond sauce, fancy cakes." Since then Rick and his wife, Deann, have created a major Mexican food enterprise, Frontera Kitchens. It includes a PBS TV series, award-winning cookbooks, a line of their own products, and two outstanding restaurants in Chicago—Frontera Grill, specializing in contemporary regional Mexican cooking, and the elegant Topolobampo.

Bayless has won numerous awards including *Food and Wine* magazine's "Best New Chef of 1988." In 1995, he won both the Beard Foundation's National Chef of the Year award and the International Association of Culinary Professionals' Chef of the Year award. Frontera Grill won the prestigious James Beard Award for Best Restaurant in the United States in 2007. The company culture of Frontera Kitchens embraces Mexican people, traditions, and food. Each year Rick takes his employees on a two-week trip to different regions in Mexico, providing his staff first-hand knowledge of the wide variety of Mexican cuisine. Through his love and respect for Mexico, Rick Bayless has elevated Mexican cuisine to an art, combining complex flavors and textures for the people of the United States.

### FROM THE EXPERTS

**Rick Bayless**

"My business is not just a money-making enterprise that I

thought was a good concept; it is an expression of my passion in life which is to bring people the food and culture of Mexico and what we can learn from it. I believe that to some extent U.S. culture is somewhat out of balance and one way we can bring balance into our lives is by learning from other cultures and we can learn a lot from Mexican culture. Mexican culture is incredibly deep and rich and has a heritage much older than ours. Looking at the indigenous cultures, their foods and how they celebrate food, you realize that the Mexicans in the U.S. offer more than unskilled labor; they come with a vast knowledge and varied experiences that enrich all. I say this to other chefs: that they have a lot to learn from the people who work in their kitchens."

## Nuevo Latino

Douglas Rodriguez, a son of Cuban immigrants, was raised in Miami. He grew up with the sights, smells, and tastes of Cuban-American cuisine and began working in his early teens at various restaurants in Miami. In 1989, at the age of 24, he opened Yuca, an upscale Cuban-style restaurant in Coral Gables, Florida. It was an award-winning success, and Douglas was a celebrated Miami chef, winning the Chef of the Year, Miami award from The Chefs of America and receiving his first and second Rising Chef of the Year nominations by The James Beard Foundation.

While Yuca served distinctly Cuban cuisine, Douglas constantly studied new flavors, ingredients, and ideas from his staff, which represents all 22 Latin American countries. Because of this, he is considered a pioneer of Nuevo Latino Cuisine.

In 1994, Rodriguez moved to New York City and became the executive chef and co-owner of the highly successful Patria. It was the birthplace for what he called "Nuevo Latino." Nuevo Latino fuses ingredients from across the Caribbean and South America into richly complex and aromatic dishes. Patria received a three-star review in *The New York Times* and accolades from *The New Yorker* and *Gourmet* among others. Currently, chef Rodriguez is the founder and executive chef in Alma de Cuba in Philadelphia, Deseo in Scottsdale, Arizona, Ola Steak in Coral Gables and Ola Miami in South Beach, Miami, and De La Costa Restaurant in Chicago.

Rodriguez is the author of *Nuevo Latino* (1995), *Latin Ladles* (1997), *Latin Flavors on the Grill* (2000), and *The Great Ceviche Book* (2003).

### Latino fusion

One of the most interesting examples of the Latinization of food is in the combinations of Latino flavors with other countries' cuisines. Because a large percentage of food preparation staffs and chefs are Latino, menus today feature roast chicken with jalapeños and yuca, jalapeño-flavored sushi, and rum cured marlin tacos. The influence of Latino spices arouses the senses and brings out the passion and excitement of food.

**FROM THE EXPERTS**

**Achy Obejas**

"I think that today everyone has tasted some form of Latin food. When I was growing up you couldn't get black beans in Indiana so you had to come to Chicago to find them. Now they are on the shelves everywhere. Taco Bell has given people an awareness and familiarity with it. Today I can make a brie and pear fajita and my guests know what a fajita is. They think the combination might be new but the fajita is not."

**Andrés Tapia**

"American food is more interesting and spicier today than it was when I first came to the U.S. I don't necessarily mean hotter, but American food is using Latin American spices. The U.S. discovered spices. Now I can find a lot more specialty spices in the regular stores."

● ● ● ● ● ● ● ● ● ● ● ● ● ● ● ● ● ● ● ● ● ● ● ● ● ● ● ●

**KEY INSIGHT**

Using celebrations, especially when marketing foods and telecommunication, creates an emotional touchstone to our heritage. The flavors, smells, and sounds of traditional dishes and the voices from our relatives abroad bring these traditions to life and create a strong emotional connection when they are done with authenticity and in non-stereotypical ways.

**LATINIZATION**

*Food Retail: Winn-Dixie Stores*

In 2006 Winn Dixie added 55 stores to its Hispanic Neighborhood Merchandising program focusing on Miami and Orlando, Florida. The 522-store chain now has 103 locations that are specifically merchandised and marketed to the Hispanic consumer, blending products and services for Hispanics into its core offerings.[3]

*Restaurants: El Pollo Loco*

"Mexican fast food restaurant chain El Pollo Loco has been sold to Trimarin Capital Partners of New York. Currently there are 328 restaurants throughout Arizona, California, Nevada, and Texas. The investment company plans to expand the

flame-grilled chicken restaurant chain nationwide with com-
pany-owned and franchise stores in Colorado, Illinois, New
England, New Jersey, New York, Oregon, and Washington,
D.C. El Pollo Loco was founded in 1975 in Mexico and the
first U.S. restaurant was opened in 1980."[4]

### Manufacturing: General Mills

At General Mills' Betty Crocker Kitchens, there is a separate
room called Cocina Betty (Betty's Kitchen) that doesn't look
like it belongs in Minneapolis. Cocina Betty, opened in 2005,
is geared toward U.S. Hispanic product development. There
are spices such as cumin, fruits including tamarinds and
guavas, and kitchen equipment such as tortilla presses and clay
pottery. *Que Rica Vida,* the company's 2006 Hispanic marketing initiative, is a food publication mailed and given away
by key retailers to 2 million Latina moms. Translated, *Que Rica
Vida* means, "What a Rich and Wonderful Life." It features con-
tent devoted to education, meal occasions, and health and
wellness. It contains recipes developed by the Betty Crocker
Kitchens, coupons, expert tips on food preparation and nutri-
tion, as well as lifestyle articles.[5]

### Products: Tortillas

According to data obtained from the market research company
Information Resources Inc., annual sales of tortillas and taco
kits are $962.9 million. Taco sales are growing at a rate 2.5
times faster than potato chip sales, according to a report
compiled by AC Nielson for the Tortilla Industry Association.
Supermarket sales of tortillas continue to rise while sales of
white bread decline.[6]

*Tortilla trends, 2006*

With the resurgence of healthy eating and a focus on overall well-ness, the tortilla industry is continuing to grow and adapt. Many tortilla manufacturers have reformulated their product to include healthful ingredients, including whole grains, and eliminate trans fats. Even the low-carb tortillas continue to sell, though many under new names, when other low-carb products have dwindled. Plus, the retail food industry's reliance on wraps as menu options has provided the tortilla industry with another stable base of con-sumers.[7]

"An annual study by the Tortilla Industry Association estimated U.S. sales at about $6 billion in 2004, double that of a decade ago. Experts projected sales to top $7 billion in 2006. In 2006 The American Tortilla Industry Association moved its headquarters from Texas to Washington, DC where it lobbies on issues such as health labeling for the whole-grain and low-fat varieties."[8]

● ● ● ● ● ● ● ● ● ● ● ● ● ● ● ● ● ● ● ● ● ● ● ● ● ● ●

KEY **INSIGHT**

The scenarios discussed above—multigenerational family gath-erings, people dancing, eating, and playing sports, scenes of very small children and senior family members together telling stories, spontaneous guitar playing and singing—all of these are natural and comfortable scenes that demonstrate a con-nection with Latino values and lifestyle. Include images of Latinos laughing and interacting with energy and spirit. These will convey passion and a celebratory view of life.

## Fashion

There are many examples in the fields of fashion, art and design that reflect Latino influences. Fashion magazines feature the elegant and sensual fashion houses of Carolina Herrera, Oscar de la Renta, Narciso Rodriguez, and the young fashion designer, Esteban Cortazar. Non-Latino designers are also using cultural cues from Latin America. Ralph Lauren showed Mariachi-inspired men's clothes in his holiday collection 2006.

## LATINIZATION

*Fashion: Guayabera*

In July 2006, the City of Miami named the guayabera its official city shirt. For the first time, the city will use guayaberas with the city seal for officials' attire at public functions as well as VIP gifts. Traditionally a man's cotton shirt with tiny pleats down the front, this shirt is worn outside the slacks and has become a "cool" fashion statement in the summer. In 2003, Lands End featured them on the cover of a summer catalogue and Donna Karen made them in 2000.

## Art

Photo: Nickolas Muray

In the art world, the ubiquity of Frida Kahlo has made her a global icon. She represents strong, courageous, intelligent, and opinionated women. Many contemporary Hispanic, Latin American, and Mexican artists fill the walls of galleries and major art museums.

Internationally known art institutions feature Latino exhibits attracting huge crowds. A couple of years ago, The Museum of Fine Arts in Houston mounted *Inverted Utopias*, the first large-scale exhibition devoted to the emergence of avant-garde art from 1920–1970 in Latin American. In 2006, the Metropolitan Museum of Art featured *Treasures of Sacred Maya Kings,* and in 2007, *Barcelona and Modernity.* Non-Latino museums are investing in and attracting crowds to a wide range of Spanish and Latin art, from pre-Colombian to contemporary. Furthermore, you see Latinization increase when names of the exhibits are now in Spanish. *Escultura Social: A New Generation of Art from Mexico City,* the summer 2007 exhibit at Chicago's Museum of Contemporary Art, highlighted recent developments including video, photography, and installations of contemporary Mexican artists from Mexico City. Concurrently, the National Museum of Mexican Art showcased *Women Artists of Modern Mexico: Frida's Contemporaries,* with work by more than 20 women artists active since the beginning of the twentieth century. During these two exhibits in Chicago, the participating museums will collaborate on a number of educational, cultural, and social programs. This was the first time the MCA and the NMMA had organized such an extensive joint program.

### FROM THE EXPERTS

**Robert Fitzpatrick**
*Pritzker Director and CEO*
*The Museum of Contemporary Art, Chicago*

"There is an increasing consciousness in the art world, universities, and museums of cultures other than our own. In the last five years there has been substantial interest in non-European exhibits—particularly work by a new generation of Latino artists. At the MCA, part of my task was to de-provincialize the museum and give it a more global prospective."

In 2006, Chicago's Mexican Fine Arts Center and Museum became the National Museum of Mexican Art. In my opinion, this institution is the premier Mexican museum in the United States. Starting in a small field house, the museum grew its physical size, but more importantly, it is now recognized nationally and internationally as a leader in the arts, giving it the cachet for its new name. One of its exhibits in 2006 demonstrated what I spoke of previously regarding our multifaceted and diverse culture with *The African Presence in Mexico*. Not only did this exhibit attract a diverse multi-ethnic crowd, but it enlightened many on the vitality and contributions of Africans across Latin America and has gone on to travel nationally and internationally.

### FROM THE **EXPERTS**

### Carlos Tortolero

"The National Museum of Mexican Art is an educational institution. It is here for all people—it is FREE and there is no charge for parking. It is here to show that every country has its own culture and it is in the Pilsen neighborhood [a Mexican neighborhood in Chicago] for people to come here and learn about our culture. It is here to teach. My father was a very smart man, but he never had the chance to get up and give a speech, but because of the Museum, I make speeches all over the U.S.

"The Museum is here as a political statement. Come here and visit our area. Learn about us; frequent our restaurants and shops. It is here to break down barriers. This museum gives people a 'chance.' It helps kids. One of the kids in our youth program had never seen a play. It was a joint summer program with the Goodman Theatre in Chicago. He impressed them so much that he was selected to play a young Scrooge in their annual production of *A Christmas Carol*."

## Design

Architecture and home design reflect the Latinization of Spanish colonial design and bold contemporary style. In contemporary design, Santiago Calatrava, the world-renowned Spanish architect, has created the Milwaukee Art Museum, the proposed World Trade Center Transportation Hub in New York City, and the proposed Spire in Chicago.

Florida, California, and the Southwest have had Spanish influenced architecture for centuries. The graceful archways, patios and gardens that are Latino influenced create places to gather and spend time with family and friends. In his book, *Casa y Comunidad*, Henry Cisneros illustrates the Latino designs that are part of our heritage.

## Sports

For decades, sports have provided entry for Latin Americans to the United States. Roberto Clemente, Pelé, and Lee Trevino were some of the early pioneers but today, Latinos fill the rosters of many sports teams. Two sports where Latino players have excelled are baseball and soccer, but there are Latino all-stars in boxing, football, tennis, swimming, and golf.

**LATINIZATION**

The July 31, 2005, issue of *The New York Times Magazine* featured an article by Jonathan Mahler on the New York Mets. The cover of this national English language magazine was bilingual, with the Spanish language boldly saying: El deporte Americano ya es un deporte latino. Cómo Omar Minaya está creando una nueva imagen del béisbol: The American game is now a Latin game. How Omar Minaya is building a baseball brand. VIVA LOS METS!

One of the most prominent and successful Latinos in béisbol is Arturo (Arte) Moreno, who bought the Anaheim Angels from Walt Disney Co. for $180 million in May 2003. Born in 1946, Moreno made his mark selling outdoor advertising and became president of Outdoor Systems. In April 2006, *Forbes* magazine estimated the team to be worth $368 million, twice the amount Moreno paid for the club only three years earlier.

Moreno's first few seasons as owner of the Angels were largely successful. The team won the American League Western Division championship in 2004 and 2005. Just prior to the start of the 2006 Major League season, Moreno scored another success in signing a lucrative contract with Fox Sports Net regarding the television broadcast rights for the Angels' regular season games. The 10-year deal significantly increased the team's television revenue.[9]

Another baseball first is Ozzie Guillén, former shortstop in Major League Baseball and the current manager of the 2005 World Series champions, the Chicago White Sox. Ozzie is the first Latin-born manager in the history of the game to have won a World Series. Ozzie has been living in and contributing to the United States for the past 26 years, and part of the Chicago landscape for 15, but he didn't have the paperwork to become a U.S. citizen. His respect for the United States was always evident in more than just his words, as one of Guillen's few team rules was to be in front of the dugout and on time for the national anthem before every game. In 2006, Ozzie and other members of his family became U.S. citizens. "This is a country that gives you so many opportunities to be what you want to be," Guillén said. "There are so many reasons you want to become a citizen, but if I explained them all, one by one, we would be here all day."

Soccer has become the leading U.S. youth sport. In 2006, the World Cup received major network coverage, opening the excitement of the sport to the mainstream. Few in the U.S. knew what the World Cup was, much less what FIFA (Fédération International de Football Association) stood for twenty years ago. During 2006, it was broadcast on ABC, ESPN, and Univision, garnering the TV channels' increased viewership and revenue. Soccer popularity has scored so well in the U.S. that we now have a 24-hour soccer channel, GolTV, featuring soccer teams from all of Latin America. Founded by three former soccer superstars, Francisco (Paco) Casals, Nelson Gutierrez, and Enzo Francescoli, GolTV has signed deals with many major U.S. cable carriers, and in 2006 signed a deal with DirecTV now reaching 7.5 million households.

**FROM THE EXPERTS**

**Andrés Tapia**

"When I came to the States from Peru for college in 1980, I played on Northwestern University's soccer team. In those days you wouldn't see soccer arcos (goal-posts) on the field. People didn't pay attention to soccer in those days here. But soccer has Latinization with an 'American twist.' I am a soccer coach for high school girls. Girls would never have played soccer in Peru, but here it is so popular, all the kids are playing. The World Cup was so much a part of my life in Peru and now I can enjoy watching it in the U.S. too!"

## Sense of humor

A sense of humor comes from shared suffering or joy. Latinos have paid a price to come to this country and our experiences are filled with events that we learn to laugh at. Each segment of the Latino population has its own fodder for jokes, whether it is El Comandante, Fidel Castro, Mexico's Vincente Fox, or Venezuela's Hugo Chavez. A number of Latino comedians such as Cheech and Chong,

George Lopez, Carlos Mencia, and now *Ugly Betty* have brought Latino humor to the U.S. mainstream. In the everyday world, whether seeing Latino chefs, gardeners, teachers, salespeople, or bankers, when you see a couple of Latinos together you'll hear and see laughter, and much of the humor comes from our fatalistic approach to life.

**FROM THE EXPERTS**

**Studs Terkel**

*Author*

"Latin American humor is special, just as all cultures have their unique humor, but the Latinos have a special view of death and an acceptance of death that is far richer."

## Passion for our heritage

Finally, Latinos have a passion for tradition and heritage. As mentioned earlier, we celebrate many of our religious traditions, but our national holidays have also become huge celebrations in the United States. Hispanic Heritage Month is one of these, although most Latinos celebrate their native-born experiences and culture all year long.

Hispanic Heritage Month is celebrated from September 15 through October 15 each year. In 1968, Congress authorized President Johnson to proclaim Hispanic Heritage Week, and twenty years later, the celebration was expanded to Hispanic Heritage Month. Today, the events begin earlier in September and end later in October, but the original dates were selected because they are significant in many Latin American countries. September 15 is the Independence Day for Costa Rica, El Salvador, Guatemala, Honduras, and Nicaragua; Mexico and Chile celebrate their independence on September 16 and September 18, respectively. As Latinos living in the U.S., we are a composite of many traditions—indigenous, Spanish, and Americanos—South, Central, and North Americans. We feel comfortable carrying two flags, as witnessed in immigration marches and Independence Day parades.

**FROM THE EXPERTS**

**Eduardo Vilaro**

"We are passionate and dramatic. Drama adds such a color to the way we do things, but it is so hard to control at times. Passion and drama are a big part of our culture. We are theatrical and have a certain penchant for drama. If you go into a Latino home you can just feel it and see it by the certain way things are arranged, the colors, textures, the style!"

## ¡Pasión!

How very Latino. We value drama, color and expression. It is all about declaring our emotions using the celebration of life, music, dance, food, art, architecture and fashion. It is our outward expression of these emotions that depict our joy and define our sorrow.

**NOTES**

1. *Hispanic Market Weekly,* "Adelante! A Special Report on the Latin Music Industry." November 13, 2006.
2. *Chicago Tribune,* "Tango and Fox Trot Make Way Back to Dance Floor." Cissy M. Rebich, January 4, 2007.
3. *www.just-food.com,* December 21, 2006.
4. *The Miami Herald,* "El Pollo Loco to Go Nationwide." August 6, 2006.

5. *www.adage.com*, August 6, 2006, New York.

6. *Snack Food & Wholesale Bakery*, "Here, There, Everywhere." Lynn Petrack, August 2006, Vol. 95, No. 8

7. *Baking Management*, "Tortilla bakers adapt to changing consumer base." August 2005, Vol. 9, No. 8

8. *USA Today*, "Tortilla biz hits the big time in America, abroad." Lynne Sladky, AP, February 12, 2006.

9. *www.wikipedia.com*

# 7

# Contribución

---

---

**THIS ENTIRE BOOK** is about the contributions Latinos are making to the United States and how Latinization is benefiting this country. In addition to the family values, determination and hard work, passion, music, food, and sports, how else are Latinos contributing to the U.S.?

## LatinoPop: The U.S. at 300 million

In October 2006, the U.S. population reached 300 million people. It only took forty years, (1966 to 2006) for the population to grow by 100 million, resulting from the net effect of births and deaths,

immigration, and emigration. A number of diverse factors deter-
mined the rate of growth, ranging from changes in U.S.
immigration laws in 1965, 1986 and 1990, to steady improvements
in life expectancy and to decreasing fertility levels. The aging baby
boom and projected growth of the white population from 2000 to
2050 at only 7 percent would mean population loss if there were
no other groups. Making up these losses, the African-American
population is projected to grow by 71 percent and the Latino population 188 percent. By 2050 Latinos will make up 24 percent of
the U.S. population.

Latinos accounted for 36 percent of the 100 million added to
the population in the last four decades, the most of any racial or
ethnic group. Immigration from Latin America and relatively high
fertility rates among Latinos were major factors in this increase.

U.S. Population at 300 Million

*percentage increase by segment, 1966–2006*

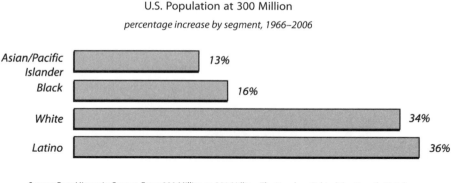

Source: Pew Hispanic Center, *From 200 Million to 300 Million: The Numbers Behind the Growth*, October 10, 2006

## Work force to sustain the aging population

How will the U.S. benefit from this growth? Latinos will contribute
the energy and muscle to sustain an aging population. Many countries throughout the 21st century world have declining
populations. Japan's population growth has declined sharply since
the 1980s. Its population figure of approximately 128 million

released in the 2005 Population Census was below the 2004 pop-
ulation estimate and marked the first time since World War II that
Japan's population decreased compared with the previous year.
Aging populations are straining government budgets throughout
Europe, as the number of workers supporting each pensioner
declines. The working-age population of Europe will drop to 57
percent in 2050, from 67 percent today, according to Eurostat, the
European Union's statistics agency in Luxembourg.

## Latinomuscle

Unlike Japan, France, and European countries where the dwin-
dling population is not being replaced by a growing immigrant
sector, the Latino population is providing muscle to the United
States that will propel this country through the upcoming decades.
As 77 million baby boomers begin to retire in the United States,
our society faces a work force deficit. Unlike other countries, we
have the hardworking Latino immigrant work force making a significant contribution and serving as our country's labor engine.
Adding to this is the higher Latino birthrate and growth of a
young population that is this country's future. Latinomuscle will
provide the fuel in every sector, but primarily in the service and
entrepreneurial sectors. The retiring baby boomers will benefit
from contributions to social security and the rest of the economy
will gain a dependable, hardworking work force.

## Skilled labor

The U.S. Department of Labor estimates that 10 to 20 million
jobs will not be filled in the next decade. Typically 70 percent of
Latinos arrive in the U.S. in their prime working age. They do not
deplete educational funds and their health is still strong, so they
are not a burden to the healthcare system. A study conducted in

2002 at Northeastern University in Boston found that during the 1990s, half of all new workers were foreign-born (Latino, Asian, etc), filling gaps left by native-born workers in both the high- and low-skill ends of the spectrum. Immigrants fill jobs in key sectors, start their own businesses, and contribute to a thriving economy.

The Pew Hispanic Center found that between 2000 and 2004, there was a positive correlation between the increase in the foreign-born population and the employment of native-born workers in 27 states and the District of Columbia. Together, they accounted for 67 percent of all native-born workers and include all the major destination states for immigrants. Further studies by Pew documented that 2006 witnessed an improved economic performance that coincided with continuing demographic growth for Hispanics. The Latino labor force and employment grew faster than for any other group.[1]

The healthy job market for Hispanic workers throughout the U.S. has been driven primarily by the construction industry. Construction contributed to nearly half a million jobs between the second quarters of 2005 and 2006, the majority of them filled by foreign-born Latinos. Since 2003, nearly 1 million Latinos have found work in construction, accounting for about 40 percent of all new jobs gained by Hispanics.

**FROM THE EXPERTS**

**Juan Andrade**

*Founder and President, the United States Leadership Institute*

"Latinos are creating new businesses at a rate three times faster than the general population, generating over 200 billion dollars per year in revenue."

In November 2005, The Institute for Latino Studies at the University of Notre Dame published an extensive report, *The State of Latino Chicago: This is Home Now*. It documented the positive impact that the more than 40,000 Mexican and Hispanic-owned businesses had in driving the economic revitalization of communities across the northeast region of Illinois. In addition, high concentrations of Latino businesses revived declining commercial districts and created prosperity in others.

U.S. entrepreneurs are often described as one of the primary drivers of the nation's economy. They contribute approximately 75 percent of all new jobs, according to the Small Business Administration. *Business Week* reports that the biggest driver within the small-business sector appears to be minority owned businesses. According to data from the U.S. Census Bureau, between 1997 and 2002, Hispanic-owned businesses grew by 31 percent, whereas the total number of U.S. businesses grew by 10 percent. The nearly 1.6 million Latino-owned businesses generated $222 billion in revenue in 2002, a 19 percent increase from 1997.

## Latino business future

*Hispanic-Owned Businesses Growth Projections for 2004–2010:*

- Hispanic-owned firms in the United States are expected to grow 55 percent to 3.2 million.
- Total revenues of Hispanic-owned firms will increase by 70 percent to more that $465 billion.
- The service and financial sectors show the largest growth.
- More than 90 percent of all Hispanic-owned firms, and their sales volume, are concentrated in 20 states.
- Together, California and Florida are home to 52 percent of all Hispanic-owned firms.

- Entrepreneurial trends and affluence among the nation's largest minority population is growing. The increase is expected to come at a robust rate of 7.6 percent annually through at least 2010.[2]

To be an immigrant, you are taking a chance. This spirit leads to an entrepreneurial state of mind, and that's what it takes to start a business. Hispanic immigrants "want to go into their own business as soon as they can leave their day jobs after saving enough money," said Michael Veve, a Washington lawyer who consults with small-business owners who want to do business with the federal government. "They seem to have a very clear perception that they can do better financially in their own businesses."

**FROM THE EXPERTS**

**Jorge Solis**
*Director, Illinois Division of Banking*

"When I see a successful Latino in business, I know that the owner has had to beat the odds. He (or she) has had to work very hard to overcome various cultural barriers that may put him at a disadvantage. At almost any cost, he has had to excel to a point that takes him above the pack. Latinos come here with the goal to be successful. He must be head and shoulders above the competition."

**KEY INSIGHT**

The primary element lacking for growth in the Latino business community is access to capital. We come from a culture where we traditionally fund business through family and friends. Access to outside capital may require a whole new way to think of money for Latino businesses. We must learn how to play the game. Lending institutions need to take a creative approach when lending to immigrant entrepreneurs. Many Latinos have not been here long enough to create an infrastructure that meets the standard financial criteria, but many banks are accepting the Matricula Consular (Mexican ID) or TIN (Tax Payer Identification Numbers) as a form of identification.

## Financial contribution: Hispanic impact on taxes

A common complaint about Latinos is that we don't pay taxes. We only burden the educational and medical resources in this country. This is a myth. Latinos pay taxes. If you own a home you pay property taxes. At work, you pay Social Security; in the marketplace you pay sales taxes. According to Justice for Immigrants, immigrants pay taxes in the form of income, property, sales, and taxes at the federal and state level. Sources vary in their accounts, but a range of studies find that immigrants pay between $90 and $140 billion a year in federal, state, and local taxes. Undocumented immigrants pay income taxes as well, as evidenced by the Social Security Administration's "suspense file" (taxes that cannot be matched to workers' names and social security numbers). The suspense file grew by $20 billion between 1990 and 1998.[3]

In June 2003, Thunderbird's American Graduate School of International Management released a study on the Mexican immigrant's financial contributions to the Unites States. Thunderbird stated, "Mexican immigrants paid nearly $600 billion in federal and sales taxes in 2002."

## Latiños: Latino youth

Latino youth are the future of the United States. One in four teens in the U.S. today is Hispanic and this segment is growing in power and influence. Between 1993 and 2001, the Hispanic teen population grew 30 percent, while the non-Hispanic population grew just 8 percent. What I call Latiños (Latino teenagers) have a projected growth rate of 62 percent by 2020 compared with 10 percent growth in the number of teens overall.[4] In 2006, the estimated 6.3 million Latiños aged 10 to 19 represented 25 percent of the entire U.S. teen population and they spent about $20 billion.[5]

● ● ● ● ● ● ● ● ● ● ● ● ● ● ● ● ● ● ● ● ● ● ● ● ● ● ● ● ●

KEY **INSIGHT**

One pertinent observation of the young Latiños I talk to today is that because of the multicultural make-up of the schools in the U.S., they don't see themselves as a minority. Clearly they are not in many places. This fact contributes to a strong sense of self and encourages young Latiños to step up and become leaders in their world.

This age group is a primary influencer in fashion, music, media, and pop culture. Caribbean guayaberas, Mexican mariachi/charro clothing details, and urban hip-hop styles appear in men's clothing. Femininity, so valued in Latinas, contributes to fashions that highlight the softer side of women. Shakira's music, hair and dance are copied by the younger generation. You can hear Spanglish, the combination of English and Spanish, as young students talk to each other or with their parents.

Similarly, Latiños are influenced by the North American lifestyle that is often in contrast to the more traditional customs of Latino families. They are pulled by the dominant American culture to be individualistic and independent while their traditional Latino family values pull at them to stay close to the collectivismo of the family. This contrasting pull of cultures can be seen in films like *Real Women Have Curves*, and the popular TV series, *Ugly Betty*. In both examples America Ferrara plays the young Latina who wants to progress in the U.S. social and career worlds while she also feels devoutly attached to her family.

### FROM THE EXPERTS

**Dr. Juan Andrade**
*Founder and President of the U.S. Hispanic Leadership Institute, recipient of the Presidential Medal*

"Today's Latino youth has the potential, but you have to stir it up. I find that you need to instill an appetite for leadership. The young Latinos today want to be effective in their own sphere of influence . . . in whatever they plan to pursue. Young Latinos are not afraid of what they may become; they won't be denied. I try to teach them that happiness comes from having a job and being effective in that job—in helping others and mentoring others."

Examining data for the decade of most concentrated change—between the 1993–94 and 2002–03 school years—The Pew Hispanic Center finds that Hispanics accounted for 64 percent of the students added to public school enrollment, while Blacks accounted for 23 percent, and Asians 11 percent. White enrollment declined by 1 percent.[6]

Yet there is a drastic contrast in educational success and attainment as young people go on to graduate from high school and college. Today, the tragically low number of Latino young people graduating from high school and college remains one of the biggest concerns of the American educational system and Latino parents who sacrifice to bring their families to the U.S. for a better life.

## Political clout

One of Dr. Andrade's priorities is voter registration. Since found-
ing the U.S. Hispanic Leadership Institute in 1982, his organization
has enrolled over 2 million new Latino voters. According to Dr.
Andrade, "Latinos are registering to vote at a rate six times greater
than the general population and turning out to vote at a rate five
times greater than the general population." This is making a
tremendous impact and will continue to do so in the upcoming
elections.

In October 2006, 17 million Hispanics were U.S. citizens over
the age of 18 and eligible to vote, an increase of 7 percent over
the 2004 election. This growing voice will add Latino leaders to
the country's roster. This constituency may have an opportunity
for the first time in U.S. history to see a Latino candidate, Bill
Richardson, a biracial candidate, Barack Obama, and a woman,
Hilary Rodham Clinton, run for President in 2008.

## Bilingualism

*Hablo Español*

I grew up speaking English as my first language, yet at the age
of six our family moved to Havana and I was introduced to the
advantages of speaking another language. It opened up a whole
new culture to me; it was like music. I was able to express myself
in another code; it was fun and trilling my r's was a game. I was
able to converse with so many more people. I have a natural affinity for language that led me to my first career, teaching Spanish.
I believe that our world expands when we learn another language.
We broaden our perspective to include other ways of seeing and
doing things and it takes us out of a self-centered universe. Learning another language is nothing short of enriching your life. As

a former Spanish teacher I encourage people to learn another language. Half a billion people in the world speak Spanish. Spanish is the second most spoken language in the United States, but any language expands your world.

● ● ● ● ● ● ● ● ● ● ● ● ● ● ● ● ● ● ● ● ● ● ● ● ● ● ● ● ●

### KEY INSIGHT

There are many Latinos in the United States today who are not comfortable speaking Spanish. They have learned "kitchen and street Spanish" but they are neither literate nor comfortable speaking grammatically correct Spanish.

When I speak to groups about this (often unacknowledged) lack of Spanish proficiency for themselves and their children, I feel and see a ripple of embarrassed recognition. To you and to anyone who feels a need to learn Spanish, I urge you to seek out the closest resource and do it ahora—now!

The rewards will be immeasurable as you begin to immerse yourself in another culture. You will discover, as Robert Fitzpatrick, the Pritzker Director and CEO of the Museum of Contemporary Art said, "There are more ways to think, to speak, to be. Anyone who has learned another language is less ethnocentric and less egocentric. Those who are monolingual and monocultural are the poorer for not knowing worlds beyond their own."

### LATINIZATION

*Manufacuring: Welch's*

In Spanish, the "ito" suffix is viewed as very sweet, endearing, and precious. Food manufacturer Welch's "Libby's Juices" used it in the name "Welchito," meaning "little Welch's." The product is really for children, with the squat can designed to fit into small hands. The graphics were redesigned with a font that's a little more whimsical, fun, and entertaining. Welch's originally launched Welchito in 1978. It was designed to meet the Puerto Rican consumer's need for an economical juice drink alternative with the long-trusted flavor and quality of the Welch's brand. Twenty-five years later Welchito is positioned for children in the United States.

*I speak English*

Another common fallacy about Latinos is that we don't want to learn how to speak English. A majority of Latinos believe immigrants have to speak English to be a part of American society and even more so that English should be taught to the children of immigrants. A Pew Hispanic Center study found, "The endorsement of the English language, both for immigrants and for their children, is strong among all Hispanics regardless of income, party affiliation, fluency in English or how long they have been living in the United States.[7]

The American Immigration Lawyers Association stated in 2003 that within ten years of arrival more than 75 percent of immigrants speak English well. Another nationally recognized organization, HACE (The Hispanic Alliance for Career Enhancement), conducts an annual professional survey. The 2006 *Latino Professional Pulse* found that Latino professionals are overwhelmingly bilingual and fully fluent in English—98 percent are English-speaking. None cited a total lack of English skills and 89 percent are fully or limited bilingual in Spanish and English. Moreover, HACE found that Latino professionals think that Spanish fluency in their careers is important and believe that it will be more important in the future.

A large percentage of people see the importance of learning a second language and believe that Spanish and Chinese are the languages to learn. Author Thomas Friedman addresses this global awareness in *The Lexus and the Olive Tree*. The globalization of the world is not a futuristic concept, and in order to participate, we all need to learn more than one language. What better way to do it than to practice Spanish and communicate with co-workers, retailers, and service people?

---

### FROM THE EXPERTS

### Aldo Castillo

"Latinos are teaching Americans the need to be bilingual. Even people who don't speak Spanish know what certain words mean such as carne asada, flan, and basic greetings such as ¡hola!"

### Carlos Tortolero

"I see that this country has an opportunity to embrace bilingualism. Compared to other countries, the U.S. is hung up about being monolingual. It is a shame that we don't value the importance of learning another language. I think Latinos are making this a real-life experience and possibility."

### Achy Obejas

"Everyone today says bodega and they know what it means. At this point so much Spanish is vernacular, like barrio, dulce de leche, caliente. Bodega used to be italicized and now it never is.

"For the glossary in my first book, *Memory Mambo*, the editors wanted to italicize the Spanish words. In my most recent book, *Days of Awe*, the Spanish is not italicized on purpose. I really didn't want to draw attention to it. When I went to Random House and said no italicized words, nobody blinked and they had no problem with it. Five years earlier, with an alternative press that was very progressive and liberal, the Spanish was italicized. The change happened between 1996 and 2001."

## The new American mainstream: A Latino middle class

A growing Latino population, business growth, a large youth population and home buying all point to a growing Latino middle class, which I call the New Latino Mainstream. This is a vibrant second and third generation segment that is maintaining its Latino heritage, language, and values. Bilingual and educated, many in this segment go on for graduate degrees and form a leadership base of Latinos in corporate America. Each year, *Hispanic Business Magazine* and *Latino Leaders* name its top 100 "Influentials," or its Leaders of the Year. They are entrepreneurs and corporate CEOs. They are also scientists, doctors, politicians, educators, and in arts and entertainment. They represent all the major Latin American nationalities that make up the Latino population. And they are young.

We are also seeing an increase in income as Hispanics become affluent faster than the overall U.S. population. A report by the U.S. Census in October 2006 reported that from 2000 to 2005, Hispanic households earning over $100,000 increased by 64 percent. All other groups grew 40 percent. Of the 2006 *Hispanic Business Magazine*'s 100 Most Influentials, 85 percent had incomes greater than $100,000 and 76 percent had graduate degrees.

## Latino leaders

There are many Latino leaders, but not nearly enough to fill the needs of corporate America today. There are also many organizations that support and develop Latino leaders such as Arquitectos, National Society for Hispanic MBAs, Society of Hispanic Professional Engineers, and Association of Latino Professionals in Finance and Accounting. The experts contributing to this book are leaders in their fields and represent the best of Latino leaders, but I'd like to introduce you to two more.

Dr. Max Gomez is a family friend. He is a distinguished media journalist with twenty-six years of on-air medical and science reporting, most recently working at WNBC TV as health and science editor. Dr. Gomez served as the medical reporter and won seven Emmys in his role as medical editor at NBC TV, CBS TV, and WNEW. He is a nationally known speaker at academic, medical and educational institutions and a regular emcee for the American Heart Association. This picture was taken at the March 2007 Heart Association Gala at the Waldorf Hotel honoring President Clinton.

Dr. Gomez's story started in Havana, Cuba where he was born in 1951. He remembers the sounds of the revolution and the exploding windows of the department store, El Siglo. What he also remembers was the interest his father, a doctor, fostered in him for science.

Max's parents divorced when he was young, and though he spent time with both his parents, he also spent many formative years with this grandparents and extended family—aunts, uncles, and cousins. When Max and his mother moved to Miami, these same family members moved from Cuba and lived with them in the U.S. "From an early age, I learned the importance of hard work, respecting my elders, and love of family. It was important to take care of family—family is always first and many U.S. corporations don't really understand that," says Dr. Gomez.

According to Max, he didn't feel that there were many barriers that kept him from becoming a leader. He excelled at Princeton, Bowman Gray School of Medicine, and Rockefeller University. Spanish is his first language but as a boy he picked up English and speaks it without an accent. A good education, bilingual skills, and an upbringing that emphasized hard work, respect, and family made Max Gomez a Latino leader.

When I asked Max to tell me about his biggest accomplishment, he said, "As a broadcast journalist, I am known as the 'voice of reason.' The media seems to have a scare of the day, whether it is anthrax or going through cancer surgery." It is the calm, informed and experienced voice of reason that garnered Dr. Gomez, the 2001 New York City Department of Public Health Award for Excellence in the Time of Crisis. Max said, "This was after September 11, 2001 and I talked people off the ledge. Of all the awards that I've won, I am most proud of that one."

Marisol Chalas, the "Dominican Fly Girl," is a Blackhawk helicopter pilot. She works at General Electric Wind Energy Division and is Company Commander in the National Guard where she leads 130 soldiers, while working on her MBA!

I met Marisol while giving the closing keynote address at the General Electric Hispanic Forum 2005 in New York City. That year General Electric gathered 450 of its top Hispanic employees to enhance their leadership skills and hear from their leaders—GE Chairman and CEO, Jeffrey Immelt, among others.

Marisol emigrated from the Dominican Republic at the age of nine. Seeing a need for more minority women in the armed forces, she became a U.S. citizen and joined her high school ROTC program. Marisol worked her way through college—logging 48 hours on the weekends alone—and became the first in her family to graduate. To do this she joined the Army National Guard because, "I didn't want to work in a factory like my parents."

This intelligent, courageous woman is one of a few Latina women to fly Blackhawk helicopters for the Army in Iraq and has received numerous military awards, decorations, and badges. Says Chalas, "As a Blackhawk trainee I was told many times that I would never get into flight school. Once at flight school I had an instructor tell me that females have a harder time learning how to fly." Marisol epitomizes the true meaning of a Latina leader and role model.


## Leadership

Our Latino cultural values teach us many things that contribute to leadership success. The first is collectivism. This we learn from the unity and devotion to family that teaches us how to work within a group, how to mentor, network, and communicate. This collective style of leadership fits into the current paradigm of leadership discussed by Thomas Friedman, *New York Times* foreign correspondent and author of *The Lexus and the Olive Tree* (1999) and *The World is Flat* (2005). Friedman describes the deconcentration of power and the democratization of decision-making. In this model there is a shared collective approach to running a company. The people closest to the consumer are more in tune with the customer's needs and therefore can provide insights not available to the CEO. Our natural Latino inclination to collectivism, learned through our families, is valued in corporate America today.

The hierarchal model of leadership has been forsaken in favor of what Stephen Covey describes as leadership developed for the good of the "whole." Dr. Stephen Covey is known for his popular book *The Seven Habits of Highly Effective People*, published in 1990. Covey identifies the habit of creative co-operation—the principle that the whole is greater than the sum of its parts, "which implicitly lays down the challenge to see the good and potential in the other person's contribution." Covey calls this habit of interpersonal leadership necessary because achievements are largely dependent on co-operative efforts with others.

**FROM THE EXPERTS**

**Sylvia Puente**

"The whole notion of leadership is different for Latinos. Starting at the top, there are very few major national Latino leaders that stand out. There is no Oprah, Martin Luther King, or Jesse Jackson as there has been in the African American community.

"Latino leadership tends to be a collective leadership, with many individual grassroots groups pulling together. A good example of this was the May 1st Immigration Marches in 2006. Hundreds of small groups came together to field millions of marchers across the United States with one clear and loud message. Latinos feel comfortable with a collective and working together they contribute to the community."

Covey and Freidman describe leadership models using concentric circles that are consistent with Latino values. The collective style of leadership gives Latinos the confidence to be leaders. Latinos also feel that our role as leaders is to help others, because of our natural commitment to community. Community service and compassion are important to the Latino community. Latino professionals care about our communities and want to give back.

• • • • • • • • • • • • • • • • • • • • • • • • • • • • • •

KEY **INSIGHT**

A good integrated marketing plan includes cause-related sponsorships. Latinos value a company that "gives back" and feel more loyal to those businesses that support Latino causes.

*HACE — Latino Professional Pulse 2006*

- Latino professionals regularly provide philanthropic support

- 58 percent give to philanthropic causes on an annual basis

- Funds are always or sometimes given to the following:
  - 72 percent to mainstream community non-profit organizations
  - 71 percent to Catholic Church
  - 67 percent to other non-profit organizations

Do you currently give philanthropic support to your community?

*493 total repsondents*

| | |
|---|---|
| NO | 41.6% |
| YES | 58.4% |

## More on Latino leadership

As Latinos we learn the values of respect, dignity, and hard work from the examples of our parents and grandparents who immigrated to this country for the sake of their families. We learn to honor diversity and the new approach it brings to ideas and problem solving. We learn that the beauty of living in the United States gives us an opportunity to progress in society, to speak our truth, and elect our leaders. The challenge for the new Latino leadership is how to own these leadership qualities in ourselves. We need to acknowledge and use these Latino qualities and learn how to reconcile them with the traditional value of humility that many of us learn from our indigenous and religious teachings.

## Contribuciones

Franklin Roosevelt, at the fiftieth anniversary of the dedication of the Statue of Liberty, said that those who landed at Ellis Island "were the men and women who had the supreme courage to strike out for themselves, to abandon relatives, to start at the bottom of influence, without money, without knowledge of life in a very young civilization."

Latinos today continue that journey and they are making the United States better because of their contributions.

**NOTES**

1. Pew Hispanic Center, August 2006, *Foreign-born Workforce and Native Born Employment,* and *Latino Labor Report, 2006: Strong Gains in Employment* Rakesh Kochhar, Associate Director for Research.
2. *Hispanic Business:* HispanTelligence
3. *Justice for Immigrants: A Journey of Hope,* The Catholic Campaign for Immigration Reform, United States Conference of Catholic Bishops Migration and Refugee Services.
4. University of Georgia Selig Center for Economic Growth, 2006.
5. Association of Hispanic Advertising Agencies, April 2006.
6. Pew Hispanic Center, October 5, 2006. *The Changing Landscape of American Public Education: New Students, New Schools,* Rick Fry.
7. Pew Hispanic Center, June 7, 2006. *Hispanic Attitudes Toward Learning English.*

# 8

# Latinization — Why it Matters

**LATINIZATION** matters quite simply because those of us who live in the United States are part of a larger community—a global community. Learning about another culture and experiencing the riches another tradition offers increases our understanding of our own place in the world. A great deal of political, economic, and social unrest is fostered by lack of understanding. When we develop an expanded view of the world we will be equipped to compete in today's global environment.

## Immigration

I started writing this book in January 2006 just as this country began hearing new debates for major immigration reform. As the year progressed we heard and voted on various approaches. These include:

- The Sensenbrenner Bill, HR 4437, a clear anti-immigrant, anti-worker approach. Among its stipulations it declared all undocumented persons to be felons along with any people who helped them. This would include hospitals, social service organizations, churches, etc.

- Senators John McCain (R-AZ) and Ted Kennedy (D-MA) sponsored a bill that offers, among other things, full legal residency to the undocumented population under some conditions.

- President Bush recommended Border Security in the form of a 700-foot wall, a guest worker program, and a lengthy legalization process.

In May 2007 as we went to press, Democrat and Republican Senators proposed a new immigration bill, supported by President Bush. It would allow the estimated 12 million undocumented immigrants arriving before January 1, 2007 to apply for legal status. They would pay $5,000, pay any back taxes, have no criminal record, speak English, and return to their native countries to apply for legal entry. There would be additional Border Patrol agents and strict employer verification of all employees. The debate continues. The point is that the immigration issue is of utmost importance in the United States today.

Latinos have been in this country for 500 years. Yet many people are afraid of increased immigration because they don't understand, relate to, or feel comfortable with a different language, style, or custom. The proposed construction of a multi-billion dollar wall will not solve the immigration issue. Who wants to live in a country behind a wall?

The reality is that most of the Hispanic population increase comes from births rather than immigration, according to Census Bureau estimates in May 2006. Sixty percent of the 1.3 million new Hispanics in 2005 were citizens because they were born here. It is the natural increase from births in Latino families here in the United States that is driving the population changes, says Roberto Suro, director of the Pew Hispanic Center.[1]

The objective of this book is to dispel the fear and highlight some of the contributions Latinos have been making for centuries. Latinization began on the coast of Florida in 1513. In the 20th century, the Hispanic population, which once consisted largely of Mexican Americans, became more diverse, through a high rate of natural growth, and a continuing inflow of Puerto Ricans, Cubans, Dominicans, and Central and South Americans.

In 1990, Latinization started to take on a larger significance. The sheer numbers make the Latino population more noticeable. Numbers have a powerful influence on patterns of behavior.

America has woven into its cultural tapestry the many traditions of immigrants, creating a richer nation as a result. This has influenced the entire country, not just the major urban entry points of Los Angeles, Miami, New York, Chicago, and Houston. In the 1990s Latinos were more likely to take up residence in the suburbs than in the city. A Notre Dame report, *The State of Latino Chicago: This is Home Now,* (November 2005) found that between 1990 and 2004, the suburban Latino population increased by more than 205 percent.

## Why does this matter?

Such diversity presents us with many new opportunities and challenges, and there are countless debates now about how diversity is or is not being embraced. How do we provide education for Latinos? Should it be different? What is a fair guest worker program that will provide the LatinoMuscle to sustain this country? How do we provide health care for Latinos? Will California lead the way?

## Soluciones

What are the solutions? We need to move past sensitivity training and beyond inclusion to embrace cross-cultural understanding. Financial institutions need to assess the new Latino entrepreneur through a larger lens, so that access to capital for the new business owners gives them an opportunity to contribute to the economy. As marketers we must refuse to "translate" messages created for an Anglo/Protestant target and develop honest communications to Latinos that speak to our values.

## LATINIZATION

*Advertising*

Toyota developed a good example of this for the 2005 Super Bowl. The 30-second spot highlighted a trend in Hispanic advertising with its bicultural/bilingual ad for Toyota's new Camry hybrid. In celebration of the diverse appeal of the big game, Toyota developed a "hybrid" commercial featuring English and Spanish to showcase the 2007 Camry Hybrid that runs on gas and electrical power.

The spot features a Hispanic father and his son driving in their new Camry Hybrid. The father explains how the new hybrid can switch back and forth between gas and electric power. His son immediately relates his family's experience to the vehicle and says, "Like you, with English and Spanish!" The father tells his son why he speaks two languages and why he bought a hybrid. He says, "I'm always thinking of your future."

"The Camry Hybrid ad represents people moving forward in their lives and creating a positive future for themselves and their families," said Jim Farley, Toyota Motor Sales vice president of marketing. "We're using a unique fusion of language and culture to introduce our new Camry Hybrid."

This is the first time Toyota has developed a bicultural, bilingual ad. With Spanish and English dialogue, the hybrid ad builds awareness with storytelling and heart-felt sentiment that resonates across cultures. Since May 2004, Toyota has ranked number one in the Hispanic market.

One idea that appears in public policy in separate locales in the U.S. is the Immigrant Welcoming Center. The Welcome Center or integration center provides information on schools, health care,

English classes, financial literacy, and citizenship. There are some versions of the Welcome Center in Illinois, the first state to propose this idea as a way to improve the status of immigrants in the state.

By developing and embracing cross-cultural understanding we see that Latinization matters because it teaches the rest of the country to appreciate Latino values—the importance of family, determination, language, and tradition. We gain a new perspective on how to relate to others. We are living in a multicultural, global world today, and we are not going back.

Thomas Friedman, in his seminal book *The Lexus and the Olive Tree* (1999), on the economics of globalization, concludes:

> "Globalization is always in the balance, always tipping this way or that. Our job as citizens of the world is to make certain that a majority of people always feel that advancing issues are leading the declines. Only then will globalization be sustainable. And no nation has a greater responsibility and opportunity to ensure this than the United States of America."

**FROM THE EXPERTS**

**Kathy Sullivan**

*President & CEO, COSI (Center for Science & Industry)*

"We need to pay attention to the 'cultural lens' we are looking though. Not all people in the U.S. grew up with the values to be individualistic, assertive, and driven. It's important to learn there is more than one way to look at people."

Our attitude about the Latinization of the United States is an advancing issue that we need to embrace. As leaders in a global society we need to remember that there is more than one way to see, to speak, to be.

**NOTE**

1. Haya El Nasser, "39 Million Make Hispanics Largest U.S. Minority Group," *USA Today,* June 19, 2003.

# 9

# Epilogue — From the Road

**AS I WAS FINISHING** the first draft of *Latinization* in December 2006, my husband Rich and I took a road trip across the Midwest to reunite with the whole family for Christmas. Driving rather than flying provided a different perspective. It was away from the chaos of holiday air travel and gave us both a day and a half to observe life away from the big city. I was not surprised to observe that Latinization is popping up all across the U.S.

We stopped in Des Moines, Iowa, at a Cracker Barrel, which for me is the epitome of "True Americana." Amid all the "cute" Christmas chotchkies and sounds of the "Little Drummer Boy," I heard the Mexican hostess speaking in Spanish to some of the wait staff. Was I surprised? No. If it had happened ten years ago, my answer would have been different.

Further along, as we clocked the mileage driving through the plains of Nebraska, we stopped in the small town of Ogallala. Adjacent to the gas station was a restaurant called La Paloma Sola Mexican Grill and Cantina (The Lone Dove).

Latinos are still immigrating to the major entry cities of Los Angeles, New York, Miami, Chicago, and San Antonio, but the real growth is in the medium-sized cities like Atlanta, Chapel Hill, and Minneapolis. This growth is spreading Latinization across the country, so you see queso blanco and tortillas in most grocery stores today and *Ugly Betty* is as popular in Denver as it is in Des Moines.

Today, rather than fear our differences, we can dignify our differences. We're lucky to be living in the 21st century.

 # The Experts

### Dr. Juan Andrade, Jr.

*President, United States Hispanic Leadership Institute*

Dr. Andrade is a Presidential Medal recipient, honored for *"the performance of exemplary deeds of service for the nation."* President Bill Clinton presented the Medal for extraordinary accomplishments in promoting civic participation and leadership development. Dr. Andrade is president of the United States Hispanic Leadership Institute. The Institute has trained over 200,000 present and future leaders, registered over two million new voters, and published 425 studies on Hispanic demographics since 1982. USHLI sponsors the largest Latino leadership conference in the nation.

## Rick Bayless

*Internationally-known authority on Mexican cuisine*

Award-winning chef-restaurateur, cookbook author, and television personality Rick Bayless has done more than any other culinary star to introduce North Americans to authentic Mexican cuisine and to change the image of Mexican food in the United States. Rick resides in Chicago with his wife Deann and daughter, Lanie. With his wife he runs award-winning restaurants, Frontera Grill and Topolobampo in Chicago. He is the founder of the Frontera Farmer Foundation, an organization that supports small local farmers and has been active in Share Our Strength, the nation's largest hunger advocacy organization. His TV program, *Mexico—One Plate at a Time* is currently in its fifth season on PBS.

## Aldo Castillo

*Art Dealer, Artist, Human Rights Activist*

A native of Nicaragua, Aldo Castillo has 24 years experience creating, managing, and developing arts and educational programs. Eight years after arriving in the United States he opened the Aldo Castillo Gallery in 1993. The gallery specializes in Latin American art, promoting established masters and emerging talent, and fostering an appreciation for all cultures through lectures, live cultural performances, and classes, inside and beyond the gallery walls.

## Henry G. Cisneros

*Founder and Chairman, CityView*

Mr. Cisneros is a former Secretary of the Department of Housing and Urban Development under President Clinton, and former president and CEO of Univision communications. Mr. Cisneros served as the first Latino mayor of San Antonio from 1981 to 1989.

He is the founder and chairman of City-View, community-building firms dedicated to producing work force homes in America's cities. CityView's mission is to work with the nation's leading homebuilders to create "villages within cities," priced within the range of average families, designed to honor community traditions, and financed to provide homeownership options for residents of the nation's cities.

## Mary A. Dempsey

*Commissioner, Chicago Public Library*

Mary Dempsey is Commissioner of the Chicago Public Library, which comprises 79 libraries with 1300 employees. Under her direction, forty new libraries have been constructed; all libraries have been equipped with state-of-the-art technology including free desktop and WiFi access to the Internet and hundreds of research databases; and book collections and innovative cultural and reading programs have been introduced in every neighborhood library. Mary holds a B.A. from St. Mary's University, an M.L.S. from the University of Illinois, and a J.D. from DePaul University. She serves as Vice Chair of the Board of Directors of DePaul University and Chair of the Urban Libraries Council.

## Robert Fitzpatrick

*Pritzker Director and CEO, The
Museum of Contemporary Art, Chicago*

An internationally recognized leader in
arts and culture, Robert Fitzpatrick was
dean of the School of the Arts at Columbia University in New York, and
previously served as president and CEO
of EuroDisney in Paris, as well as president of California Institute of the Arts
from 1975–1987. He also served as vice
president of the Los Angeles Olympic Organizing Committee and
director of the 1984 Olympic Arts Festival, and later founded and
directed the Los Angeles Festival.

## Henry Godinez

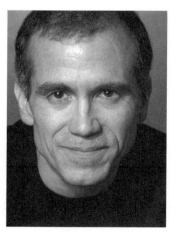

*Resident Artistic Associate,
The Goodman Theatre, Chicago*

As director of the Goodman's Latino Theatre Festival, Mr. Godinez's productions
include José Rivera's *Cloud Tectonics* as
well as *Zoot Suit, Mariela in the Desert,
Electricidad, Straight As A Line, Millen-
nium Mambo, Psst...I Have Something to
Tell You Mi Amor, Anna in the Tropics,*
and six seasons of *A Christmas Carol.*
Godinez has acted at the Goodman, Chicago Shakespeare, Court
Theatre, Apple Tree Theatre, Victory Gardens, Wisdom Bridge, and
The Old Globe Theatre. He is an associate professor in the Department of Theatre at Northwestern University.

## Juana Guzman

*Vice President, National Museum of Mexican Art*

Native Chicagoan and an arts activist for over twenty-five years, Juana Guzman has been serving as vice president of the National Museum of Mexican Art since 1999. Before coming to the museum, she served for twenty years as the director of Community Cultural Development for the city of Chicago's Department of Cultural Affairs. At the DCA, Ms. Guzman created the Chicago Coalition of Community Cultural Centers, a partnership of sixty non-profit arts organizations and developed the nationally acclaimed Chicago Neighborhood Tours.

## Carlos R. Hernandez

*Executive Director, Puerto Rican Arts Alliance*

Mr. Hernandez is a co-founder of the PRAA and he directs all cultural programming, development, and planning for the organization. Since 1998, the PRAA has staged the Cuarto Festival, featuring Puerto Rico's unique guitar instrument. This concert is the largest Puerto Rican cultural event in the Midwest. Hernandez is the recipient of the prestigious 2005 Dr. Jorge Prieto, Sr. Humanitarian Award, bestowed during Hispanic Heritage Month. In 2006, Mr. Hernandez received the Citibank Hispanic Heritage Award for his contributions in the art field.

## Achy Obejas

*Author*

Born in Havana, Achy Obejas is a respected journalist and a critically acclaimed, award-winning author. Her books include *Days of Awe, Memory Mambo* and *We Came all the Way from Cuba So You Could Dress Like This?* Her poems, stories and essays have appeared in dozens of anthologies, including Akashic's *Chicago Noir.* A longtime con-

tributor to the *Chicago Tribune,* she was part of the 2001 investigative team that earned a Pulitzer Prize for the series, "Gateway to Gridlock." Her articles have appeared in *Vanity Fair, Village Voice, The Nation, Playboy,* and *MS,* among others. Currently, she is a music contributor to *The Washington Post* and the Sor Juana Writer in Residence at DePaul University in Chicago.

## Sylvia Puente

*Director, The Center for Metropolitan Chicago Initiatives of The Institute for Latino Studies, University of Notre Dame*

Ms. Puente's mother introduced her to a life of activism at 13, when she joined her first picket line supporting the United Farm Workers. In 2003, she was one of 25 Chicago-area women named a "Pioneer for Social Justice." In 2005, Ms.

Puente was selected one of the "100 Most Influential Hispanics in the U.S." by *Hispanic Business Magazine.* She is a leading public policy analyst on issues impacting Latinos. At the Institute for Latino Studies, she works tirelessly on community research, promotes community capacity-building, and speaks on issues that affect Latinos.

# Jorge Solis

*Director, Illinois Division of Banking*

Formerly responsible for Middle Market Hispanic Banking, and a number of not-for-profit lending relationships at LaSalle Bank N.A. He focused on all aspects of commercial banking for middle-market companies with specific emphasis on Hispanic-owned, privately held entities. His responsibilities included formulation and implementation of plans and strategies with a primary goal to make LaSalle Bank N.A. the leading financial institution serving this market with commercial lending, private banking, treasury management, and capital market products. Currently, Mr. Solis is responsible for regulating Illinois' banking and residential mortgage industries.

# Kathryn D. Sullivan, Ph.D.

*President and CEO, COSI*
*(Center of Science & Industry)*

Dr. Sullivan is the first American woman to walk in space and a veteran of three NASA shuttle missions. She first launched from Kennedy Space Center on October 5, 1984, with a crew of seven. In 1993, Dr. Sullivan left NASA to accept a Presidential appointment as Chief Scientist at the National Oceanic and Atmospheric Administration. Here she oversaw programs ranging from climate and global change to satellites and marine biodiversity. In 2004, Sullivan was inducted into the Astronaut Hall of Fame. At COSI, Dr. Sullivan ignites in others a passion for the wonder and importance of the sciences.

## Andrés T. Tapia

*Chief Diversity Officer/Emerging
Workforce Solutions Leader,
Hewitt Associates*

Andrés Tapia is Hewitt Associates' Chief
Diversity Officer/Emerging Workforce
Solutions Leader, responsible for leading
the company in its internal and external
diversity vision. Using his training and
experience in journalism, history, political science, and HR he has created
innovative approaches to the firm's attraction, retention, and development strategies to foster an inclusive working environment.
Working closely with Hewitt's CEO on business and people strategies, he developed a three-pronged strategy to increase value to each
of the firm's stakeholders—associates, clients, investors, and communities through diversity and inclusion.

## Studs Terkel

*Author*

Born in 1912 in New York City, Studs
Terkel is a prize-winning oral historian,
author and radio personality. He grew up
in Chicago and graduated from the University of Chicago with a law degree, but
Terkel became famous using his inter-
locutory skills as an interviewer in radio rather than a lawyer. He is
well known for *The Studs Terkel Program* that aired on WFMT Radio
for forty-five years. Studs Terkel is a keen observer of people. His
books of oral history interviews began with *Division Street: America*
followed by *Hard Times, The Good War,* and *Race.* In 2001 he published, *Will the Circle Be Unbroken: Reflections on Death, Rebirth,*